American Healthcare

The Economics of American Healthcare explores economic growth and the health sector. Is the health sector a curse or a blessing? The American health sector now accounts for an estimated 20% of the economy and will likely increase even more in the coming years. American healthcare spending and healthcare spending per capita far exceed that of other developed countries. Yet our health, as measured by life expectancy and infant mortality, is relatively poor by comparison with the developed world. Other measures of quality, including hospital-acquired infection and other medical errors, are too common. Healthcare costs still financially cripple households despite advances associated with the Affordable Care Act. There is widespread dissatisfaction with the American healthcare system and growing support for more change. It is also the case that the health sector has been a leader in the evolution of the US economy. The history of economic development is largely attributable to the integration of new technology. We tend to applaud new technology and the improvement it brings to our lives. Important new technologies often grow rapidly and faster than the economy as a whole. This leads to larger shares of the economy. Advancements in technology have evolved rapidly, and while there is an appreciation that these technologies are an engine of economic growth there is considerable apprehension about the costs and associated benefits and how this will impact the economy. This book details important health-sector institutions and perhaps uniquely explores linkages between healthcare and broader economic growth. It also explores asymmetric information and the nature of competition in the health sector. Special attention is paid to monopoly power in labor markets in healthcare that contributes to inefficiencies in the system. The author also discusses cost-effectiveness and allocative efficiency as well as productivity and cost. Policy recommendations for improved efficiency in the long run are also provided.

Contents

Figures

Foreword

When my friend and former mentor, Dr. Peter Hilsenrath, mentioned he was working on a book about the American healthcare system, I was impressed with his willingness and audaciousness to try to comprehensively examine and effectively relay to readers the evolution and current challenges of a system as complex and opaque as our healthcare system. This is a very tall order for any author.

To successfully carry out this, it requires an author to have a few key attributes. Among them, first, one needs to have built up a lifetime of knowledge and experience in working on healthcare issues and interacting with all levels and stakeholders of the healthcare system. Second, the author must be a very astute observer with the curiosity to seek to understand why the American healthcare system has its present design and why it sometimes seems to be immovable in its apparent inefficiency and inequity. Finally, it helps if the author is an economist or at least has an economics perspective. You should know that I, myself, am an economist and, thus, this statement might be considered the typical arrogant assertion that an economist might just make. (Be aware that I also received my PhD from the University of Chicago, which is viewed by some as the center of self-centeredness among schools of economics.)

However, although this last attribute is partly tongue-in-cheek, I'm also serious about the value of having an economics lens to view the American healthcare system with. Without this economics lens, it is difficult to fully recognize and understand the implications of market failures and often unfortunate incentives that have become institutionalized within the American healthcare system. Economics is not about tabulating the accounting cost of a procedure or a healthcare system. Economics is about understanding the range of feasible options faced by stakeholders participating in the system and understanding each option's *economic* cost vs. benefit from the perspective of those stakeholders. Doing this, we increase understanding of each stakeholder's incentives and, thus, elucidate why they seem to take the actions they do. Economic cost and benefit themselves are not narrow monetary accounting terms but have an expansive, sometimes almost philosophical breadth to them. Sometimes they are unquantifiable. However, it is the economist's job to understand both why actors within the system behave the way they do given their range of options and corresponding costs and benefits, and, in turn, why their past actions led to the evolution and maintenance of the current system, despite the fact that the system seems incredibly inefficient, unsustainable in light of our aging demographics, and socially unjust, and in much need of transformation. A critical qualifier to my assertion on the need for this economics lens, though, is that this is not sufficient by itself to lead to a deep understanding of the American healthcare system. It must be paired with an open mind toward incorporating insights and feedback from the multiple, often competing and dynamic perspectives and disciplines involved within and outside of the healthcare system.

Peter has all these attributes and then some, and the impressive scope, balance, and quality of this book reflects this. I am a Professor of Economics and Population Health Sciences with the University of Utah, and I also lead the Matheson Center for Health Care Studies. I've spent my entire academic career working as a health economist and engaging with many of the issues highlighted in Peter's book. In fact, I started out my career working with and learning from Peter. Even with all that, I learned quite a few more things I didn't realize or fully appreciate about the American healthcare system.

In the book, Peter starts with providing an expansive and fascinating overview of healthcare from prehistory to the present day. Afterward, the book presents the historical evolution of each component within the American healthcare system including the healthcare professions and the hospital and 3rd party payer systems as well as the healthcare regulatory environment. The book methodically describes and discusses the challenges that have arisen as our healthcare system evolved over this time. There is a superb exploration of efficiency, cost-effectiveness, and productivity in healthcare. Peter takes the reader from a historical and micro-view of the American healthcare system to a broad macro-view and discusses the multiple crosscurrents that the system is currently dealing with as it struggles to address high cost of care balanced against the growing long-term healthcare needs of the aging population and the long-standing challenges of healthcare inequity and social determinants of health. The discussions of the healthcare system within the context of US price inflation and economic inequality are particularly interesting and important given current events. Overall, the book has a refreshing tone of optimism, not the usual exasperation or cynicism that often comes up when discussing healthcare, and it concludes by giving us hope of a transformation of the American healthcare system that is ultimately powered by technological innovation.

I also want to say that Peter's writing style is clear and lively, a pleasure to read. (It is worth noting that Peter's editor for the book, Jim Hill, earned a PhD in English from the University of Iowa, where he went on to become a writer and editor in the school's Department of Health Management and Policy.) Economists are notorious for their long-winded, dry and dense prose, but this book does an exceptional job of clearly relating concepts and details in an easy-to-follow and engaging way for a broad audience. This is a very balanced and thought-provoking book that should be required reading for anyone interested in deepening their understanding of what's going on and what is likely to happen with the American healthcare system. It discusses topics that are either superficially covered or not covered at all in prior books. The American healthcare system is one subject that everyone living in the US should be highly invested in learning more about. Everyone here will have either direct experience with trying to navigate the healthcare system or will have loved ones who have dealt with aspects of it. Peter's book will give foundational knowledge and context to help people become more informed consumers and advocates for healthcare. For those not residing in the US, this book is equally valuable in providing an in-depth, comparative insight into the perplexing system that is American healthcare. In my opinion, this book will quickly become a key book within healthcare education, and I very much look forward to using it in my own courses and recommending it to my students and colleagues.

Fortunately, Peter was audacious enough to take on this subject, and he has written a book that will be an invaluable resource and textbook in the study of the American healthcare system.

Fernando A. Wilson, PhD
Governor Scott M. Matheson Endowed Chair in Health Care Studies
Director, Matheson Center for Health Care Studies
Professor of Economics and Population Health Sciences
University of Utah

Preface: Institutions

The term "institution" has several meanings. It can refer to an organization with an important social function, such as a church, or to a facility that provides specialized care, such as a hospital, or financial services, such as a bank. The term can also refer to abstract entities such as established customs, laws, and practices: Private property, for example, and marriage and religion are all institutionally embedded in our society. Such institutions are foundational and evolve over time, shaped by dynamic historical forces, including social, political, economic, environmental, and technological changes. Accordingly, institutions are best understood from a multidisciplinary social science perspective. To that end, in writing this book about Healthcare and how it developed, I have used perspectives from history, economics, and other related fields. The reader will find the style of writing largely eschews jargon and technical analyses, or attempts to minimize it, and as a result, the discussion is, I think, an easily grasped exploration of important elements of this sector of the economy—elements that set it apart from other sectors and give it a special social dispensation.

A key reason healthcare occupies a special place in the economy is the commonly held view that Americans have a right to at least basic health services. In this respect, healthcare is partially a public good in which the entitlement of all provides wider social utility. A second reason has to do with the agency afforded to healthcare providers to use their expertise on behalf of patients. The health sector is not unique in this regard, but it has adapted unique institutions to accommodate the agency of healthcare providers.

The American healthcare system, complex and costly in the extreme, has long been a focus of social and political attention. It is a worry and a blessing at the same time. On the one hand, costs are high and a major source of concern. On the other hand, the health sector is an engine of growth, generating new technologies with long-run economic potential and profound human benefit. What are we to make of this? How do we parse conflicting narratives?

I have arranged the chapters of this book in three parts. In the three chapters of the first part, I discuss the evolution of healthcare and its institutions, exploring its deep roots as a way to better understand contemporary institutions. The second part addresses conventional topics in health economics such as asymmetric information, monopoly power, occupational control, health insurance, and application of cost–benefit and cost-effectiveness analyses—all important elements in driving the high cost of American healthcare. The final section integrates the health sector with macroeconomics, addressing productivity and costs, inflation, and economic growth and finally looking ahead to consider how the health sector will shape economic development going forward.

One of my aims in writing this book is to encourage in the reader a greater appreciation of cost structure in healthcare and the potential of the health sector to achieve lower costs and also serve as an engine of efficiency, growth, and development in the coming decades. The audience of the book is a general one—anyone with interests in economics and healthcare—but it is also for those with backgrounds in economics, healthcare management, and the health sciences.

Acknowledgments

I owe a debt of gratitude to others in the production of this book. Their timely review and commentary were an important part of the process. I would like to thank Allan Bennett, PhD, CFA of Winchester Virginia and Phil McCarthy, MBA of Campbell, California, for their review, comments, and support. I also want to express my appreciation to Peter Hoenigsberg of North Andover Massachusetts for valuable advice. Special recognition is warranted for Jim Hill, PhD of Coralville, Iowa, for outstanding editing. I want to extend my thanks to my wife Grace for her patience and support in this project. I also want to thank the University of the Pacific for providing a sabbatical, which helped afford the time necessary to bring this book to fruition, and to Veronica Wells, Professor in Pacific's main library, who also helped.

About the Author

Peter Hilsenrath received his BA in economics and environmental studies from the University of California at Santa Cruz and PhD in economics from the University of Texas at Austin. He held the Joseph M. Long Chair in Healthcare Management and Economics at the University of the Pacific and is now Professor Emeritus. He was Professor and founding Department Chair of Health Management and Policy at the University of North Texas Health Science Center in Fort Worth. Earlier, Dr. Hilsenrath was an Assistant and then Associate Professor at the University of Iowa, first in the College of Medicine and later in the College of Public Health. He also held faculty appointments in the Economics Department at the University of the Witwatersrand in Johannesburg, South Africa.

Additionally, Dr. Hilsenrath has held nonacademic positions. He served as Chief Economist for Syfrets Managed Assets in Cape Town and was on the Research Staff at the Center for Naval Analyses in Alexandria, Virginia.

Peter has taught courses about finance, management, and economics in the health sector. He has also taught courses in ethics and corporate social responsibility as well as natural resource economics. Peter's research is wide-ranging. He has published over 75 peer-reviewed articles and reports. They include publications in medical, management, and economics journals such as the *American Journal of Public Health, American Journal of Roentgenology, Archives of Pediatrics & Adolescent Medicine, Defence & Peace Economics, Health Care Management Review, Journal of Management History, Journal of Rural Health,* and *Technology in Society.* Many of his papers address issues of efficiency in the health sector. He has also published in *Business Day (South Africa), China Daily, Fortune, Huffington Post, Jerusalem Post,* and *The Wall Street Journal.* He has served on Editorial Boards for *Hospital Topics, International Journal of Pharmaceutical and Healthcare Marketing, Journal of Health Administration Education,*

Journal of Health Care Finance, Inquiry: The Journal of Medical Care Organization, Provision and Financing, Journal of Primary Care & Community Health, and *The Journal of Rural Health.*

Dr. Hilsenrath has presented his work at many national and international conferences as well as in important institutions such as the Pentagon and South Africa's Parliament. He has participated in funded projects from organizations that include the Centers for Disease Control, the US Agency for Health Care Policy and Research, and the US Department of Education.

HISTORY AND
EVOLUTION

Chapter 1

Origins and Evolution of Healthcare

Prehistoric Healthcare

Health is perhaps our most treasured asset, evident in the great lengths we go to in safeguarding our well-being and that of our loved ones. Our generation is notable for the scope of resources we are willing to spend on health services. The level of technology in healthcare today simply does not compare with anything in the past, and it is certainly the case that modern healthcare affords services unimaginable in earlier times. But health services have been an important part of the economy and social fabric for millennia.

We know that *Homo sapiens* and others from our evolutionary tree cared for one another for hundreds of thousands of years, but little is known of their medical technology. We believe, for example, that our forebears used herbal and other natural remedies—that they ingested clay to absorb toxins and, topically, to fight infections and treat wounds. (Use of clay is not unique to humans as other primates and birds ingest clay.) Moreover, chimpanzees and other apes are known to eat trichome plants to combat parasites, and perhaps early humans did this as well. Certainly, there is evidence of prehistoric people using birch bark as a laxative and setting broken bones. Such simple physical measures were usually combined with spiritual intervention, which was overseen by the tribal medicine man or shaman.

A common intervention in human prehistory was trepanning, which involved cutting, drilling, or scraping a hole in the skull. An example of one such skull is shown in Figure 1.1. Trepanning was done, it is thought, to relieve cranial pressure after an injury as well as to treat mental illness, and it is believed to have been

DOI: 10.4324/9781003186137-2

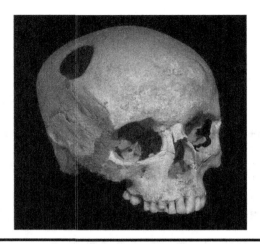

Figure 1.1 Trepanned Skull

Source: File: Trepanned skull of a woman-P4140363-black.jpg—Wikimedia Commons

Author: Rama

Creative Commons 3.0

ritualistic in many cases, though little is understood of the context of such practices. Trepanned skulls have been found dating back 7,000 to 8,000 years.

Evidence of this remarkable medical procedure has been found in different locations scattered around the globe, including Europe, China, Siberia, North and South America, Africa, and Polynesia. The excavated skulls show that many of these trepanned "patients" survived, at least for a time; most are from men, perhaps because men were more likely to be injured in battle or otherwise. In any case, the surgical ability of our ancestors and the endurance of these patients should humble our own sense of medical prowess.

The Ancient World Egypt

In ancient Egypt, one of the great early civilizations, much was understood about the human body and maintaining its health. The Nile River, a pillar of Egyptian civilization, was a key water source to support agriculture and livestock, but less well known was the use of the Nile for washing and hygiene. No doubt it had a role in public health practices via toilets, a convenience for wealthier Egyptians, and was also used to dispose of sewage, which of course undermined public health downstream.

Egyptian medical practices spread beyond Egypt's political reach as historical evidence shows. The borders of ancient Egypt varied over the millennia, at times including parts of what is now Sudan, South Sudan, and Israel, as shown in Figure 1.2. The Old Testament describes close ties between Canaan and Egypt. There is historical evidence to support this. Some medical practices may have spread. Circumcision, for example, was commonly practiced in ancient Egypt (as well as other cultures of the ancient Middle East including Mesopotamia), and this is thought to have been done at least partially for hygienic reasons. The practice has endured and remains widespread among Muslims and Jews.

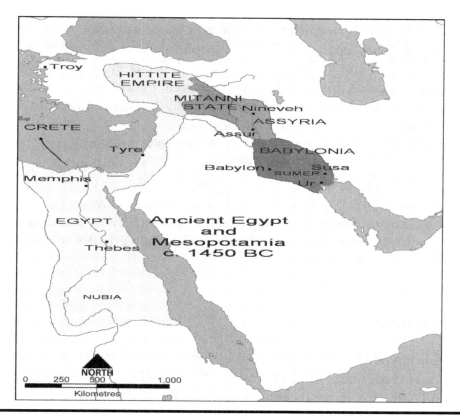

Figure 1.2   Ancient Egypt and Mesopotamia, c. 1450 BC

Source: https://commons.wikimedia.org/wiki/File:Ancient_Egypt_and_Mesopotamia_c._1450_BC.png

Author: Svift

Creative Commons CC0

Religion and medical care in the ancient Middle East were usually integrated to some extent, infusing healing and health with a spiritual overlay. Medicine was commonly taught in religious settings and healthcare providers remained tied to these communities. They were in some respects like "medicine men" in native American culture or "witch doctors" in southern Africa. Like them, the ancient Egyptians had hundreds of medical and health-related drugs and products. We know of such unguents and palliatives from translations of hieroglyphic writing on papyrus; thanks to the translations made possible by the Rosetta Stone (discovered in 1799), scholars were able to unlock the hieroglyphics, opening a window to medicine and health in the world of the pharaohs.

We have learned that the ancient Egyptians used copper salts and honey combined with grease as antiseptics. (Honey is quite resistant to bacteria.) They concocted mouthwashes with mint and other ingredients as a remedy for bad breath. They used aloe for burns, opium and thyme for pain, and even toothbrushes and toothpaste for oral hygiene. They also used adhesive bandages for wound care. Perhaps, the first great dentist of ancient Egypt was Hesy-Ra of the third dynasty; other notable dentists followed in what became a long tradition of Egyptian dentistry.

Mummification was an art as well as a science in ancient Egypt. Professionals who practiced it used specific medical compounds, special surgery, and wrapping and stitching techniques with great skill. This coincided with the development of surgical tools and advances in the understanding of human anatomy. So skillful were the experts in mummification, the remains of Ramses II are remarkably well preserved after more than 3,000 years, as shown in Figure 1.3.

Mesopotamia

Along with Egypt and the empire of the Hittites, Mesopotamia was a great ancient civilization. Centered on the Tigris and Euphrates rivers, as shown in Figure 1.2, it expanded at times to influence a much wider area. Medicine was closely integrated with religion and spirituality among the Mesopotamians, just as it was among the Egyptians. Its Code of Hammurabi, from the 2nd millennium BC, offers us a window into that long-ago world of healthcare in which, for example, price discrimination was routine (i.e., different prices are charged for different classes of consumers). This practice effectively segregates consumers by income group. In ancient Mesopotamia

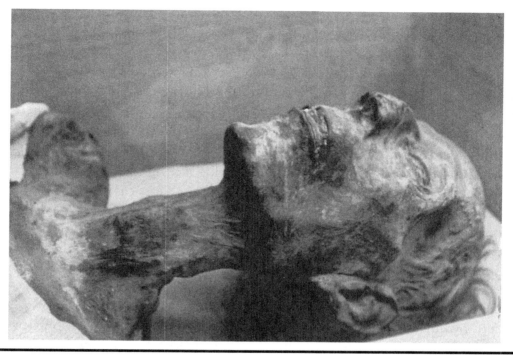

Figure 1.3   Mummified Remains of Ramses II: 1279–1213 BC

Source: https://commons.wikimedia.org/wiki/File:RAMmummy.jpg

Creative Commons CC 3.0

medical prices were highest for well-to-do citizens and lowest for slaves, which, interestingly, finds a parallel today in the United States: Here, the highest prices are associated with wealthy consumers and their generous health insurance plans while some of the lowest prices are found in Medicaid programs for lower-income Americans. We also know Mesopotamians imposed penalties on medical practitioners for poorly executed work, some of which could be quite harsh. Medical practices then were similar to many today, including simple surgery, use of plaster casts, and bandaging. As in Egypt, hygienic practices were recommended for improved health.

Greece and Rome

Among the ancients, Greece and Rome are most responsible for establishing the medical foundations of healthcare in the United States. The influence is so strong that Latin was required in the curriculum for medical students until the second half of the 20th century, and much existing medical terminology is derived from Greek or Latin.

The Greek physician Hippocrates (460–370 BC) is considered to be the father of Western medicine. He helped establish a scientific approach to medicine, which included a careful study of the manifestations of disease, the influence of diet and environment, and the use of clinical histories. It was doctors, Hippocrates maintained, not just the gods, who could understand and treat health issues and provide a prognosis for medical conditions. He performed early work on draining chest cavities as well as on treating hemorrhoids. An important early medical book, the *Hippocratic Corpus*, is associated with him (although it is believed to have multiple authors), and here is found the Hippocratic oath, a ritual that medical and other healthcare students routinely take upon graduation. It commits the graduate to a lifetime of ethical practice. One aspect, with important ramifications today, is a commitment to do whatever possible to improve patient health. Among the modern variations is the promise to "apply, for the benefit of the sick, all measures [that] are required, avoiding those twin traps of overtreatment and therapeutic nihilism." This can be interpreted as providing care when it is helpful but refraining when it is not. Nowhere in the oath, however, is the concept of economic efficiency stated, in which overtreatment is defined as excessive cost relative to benefit. From a modern perspective, this absence appears as a gaping hole in the ethical identification of how much care is too much. It is where healthcare providers and health economists commonly part company. In a world where healthcare institutions are becoming more market like, it is particularly problematic for those who are not prepared to use cost and economic criteria because markets do.

Even though the modern world owes much to early Greek medicine, the ancients had certain misconceptions that have had serious consequences. For example, the ancient Greeks and Romans believed in humorism, which entails belief in the importance of balance between bodily fluids: blood, phlegm, black bile, and yellow bile. These in turn were associated with air, water, earth, and fire, respectively. Treatments using the theory of humors might have recommended exercise and diet, quite benign measures, but others such as bloodletting, emesis, or use of enemas could be counterproductive. The theory of humorism in Western medicine continued through the 18th century and into the 19th century. George Washington's death, in 1799, is sometimes attributed to misplaced humorism. To treat a bad sore throat, the ex-President's chief aide called for his doctors, who were skilled at bloodletting. Washington died after they drained 40% of his blood.

Another great physician from the world of ancient Greece and Rome was Galen of Pergamon, who lived from 129 to around 210 AD. Galen advanced the understanding of human anatomy by means of dissections of monkeys and pigs—human dissection was generally frowned upon as the human body was considered inviolate. Such prohibitions persisted in Europe until the later Middle Ages. In Hellenic Alexandria, however, important advances in knowledge of human anatomy occurred, which provided physicians a better grasp of the nervous system, the eye, and the heart (with its component chambers and valves).

Galen also put forward a theory of blood circulation. But extrapolating from the dissection of animals to human structures and processes had its limits, and as a result, his theory contained errors. Blood circulation in humans was not really understood until the 13th century with the scheme of pulmonary circulation advanced by Ibn al-Nafis of Damascus. Galen also served as a physician to gladiators in Pergamon and acquired a reputation for great competence as only five gladiators died under his four years of service. He later served as a physician to Roman emperors Marcus Aurelias, Commodus, and Septimius Severus.

Some symbols of Hellenic medicine persist in the present day, such as the snake of Asclepius. The Greek god of medicine, Asclepius was the son of Apollo; his daughters included Hygeia, the goddess of cleanliness, and Panacea, the goddess of universal remedy. His snake-entwined staff, known as the Rod of Asclepius, is included in the World Health Organization logo, as shown in Figure 1.4.

Figure 1.4   Rod of Asclepius

Source: https://commons.wikimedia.org/wiki/File:World_Health_Organization_Logo.svg

Byzantine and Islamic Contributions

The world of late antiquity in Europe was a period of great ferment and a time when one might have expected a halt to advancement in human medicine as the dark ages approached. To sketch just a few political and cultural changes: Christianity gained as a countervailing force against Hellenistic values, especially in the 3rd and 4th centuries. At the same time, much of the western Roman Empire became weakened and subject to invasion by various tribes including Vandals, Goths, and Huns. These conditions contributed to Constantine the Great's conversion to Christianity and his decision to move the Roman capital to Constantinople. The eastward shift was associated with the gradual erosion of Latin and the ascendency of Greek in what became the Eastern Roman Empire and later the Byzantine Empire. Rome fell in 476 but Byzantium endured until 1453, nearly a millennium later.

The Byzantine Empire reached its territorial zenith (shown in Figure 1.5) under the reign of Justinian when an attempt to reestablish

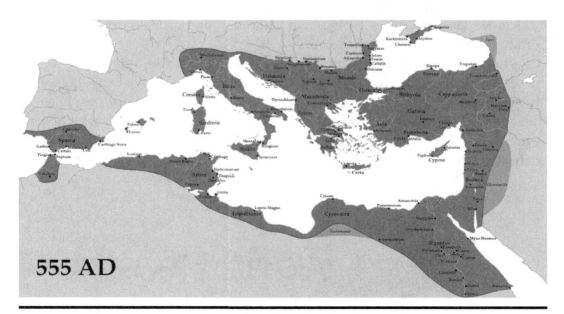

Figure 1.5 Map of Byzantium at the Time of Justinian

Source: http://en.wikipedia.org/wiki/Byzantine Empire#/media/File:Justinaian555AD/png

Author: Tataryn

Creative Common CC 3.0

rule in the West was undertaken in the 6th century. This expansion was undermined by an outbreak of the Black Plague, which became known as the Plague of Justinian, the first recorded outbreak of *Yersinia pestis*, the plague pathogen. The extent and severity of the epidemic are debated by historians, but we do know that it devastated Constantinople and is thought to have seriously weakened the army. Justinian himself contracted the disease but survived. Procopius, a noted contemporary historian, describes a death toll of 10,000 per day in the city; the conditions were horrific. Some historians see its impact rivaling that of the Black Plague of the 14th century and speculate that it facilitated the socioeconomic conditions from antiquity into the medieval period. It is thought to have disproportionately impacted the more urban and Romanized communities as far afield as Britain.

After the fall of Rome, Western Europe entered the early Middle Ages, few people read Greek, and familiarity with Latin was largely limited to the Church. Knowledge of medicine was more secure in the Byzantine Empire; Greek learning survived there as Greek was the native language. Knowledge is even advanced in some cases. *The Medical Compendium in Seven Books* by Paul of Aegina, written in the late 7th century, was an important contribution and was widely used in the Middle Ages and beyond. It improved classical learning in several areas of medicine, including the use of urinary catheters, tracheotomy surgery, and spinal and hernia repairs.

The Eastern frontier changed radically in the 7th and 8th centuries as the Islamic World exploded onto the scene and replaced the Sassanid Persians. The Abbasid caliphate seized much of Byzantium's territory in the Middle East, as shown in Figure 1.6. Although political barriers existed between the Byzantines and the newly established Islamic domains, there was substantial trade. Such contacts spread medical knowledge of the Greeks and Romans to Bagdad as well as other centers in the Arab and wider Muslim world. These centers cultivated the acquisition and preservation of knowledge from earlier times, including the medical and health sciences of the ancients. Like the Byzantines, Islamic scholars made substantial advances in medical knowledge. Advancements were made in ophthalmology, with improvements in the treatment of cataracts and trachoma. Also, there were developments in the treatment of pain, for example, via extracts from poppies.

A noted Islamic medical figure was Avicenna. Born near Bukhara, in present-day Uzbekistan, he became a leading medieval scholar in the 11th century. Many of his works survive including 40 on medicine; his *Canon on*

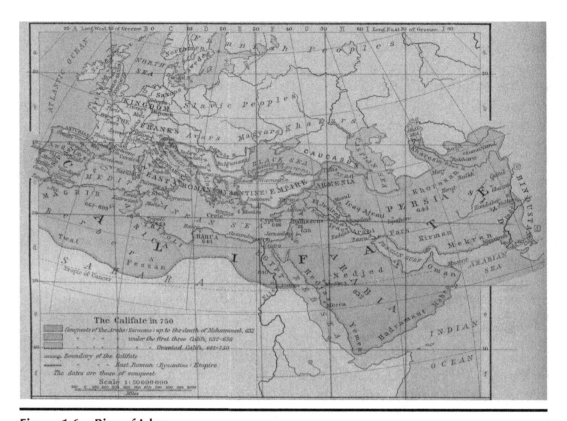

Figure 1.6   Rise of Islam

Source: https://legacy.lib.utexas.edu/maps/historical/shepherd/califate_750.jpg

Courtesy of the University of Texas Libraries, The University of Texas at Austin

Medicine, for example, remained an important text for centuries. He theorized about airborne diseases, promoted the use of forceps in childbirth, and made contributions to the treatment of heart and kidney diseases. Another great Islamic scholar, previously noted, was Ibn al-Nafis who discovered pulmonary circulation in the 13th century. Some years later, in the 17th century, the English physician to James I, William Harvey, advanced this theory and was widely credited with this discovery in the West, until very recently when the historical record was corrected. It is known that Harvey studied in Padua, Italy, where much of the medical knowledge of the Islamic World had been rediscovered and was available.

Another major contribution of the Byzantines is hospitals. Hospitals were known in early medieval Europe, for example, the Hotel-Dieu (Hotel of God) in Lyon founded by Childebert I, King of the Franks in 542 AD., which provided care and some treatment. The Byzantines, however, took the institution to another level. They capitalized on the medical knowledge of the ancients and developed larger and more well-run hospitals than had existed to date. At one time, there were an estimated 160 hospitals in the empire. Perhaps, the most well-known today, whose records survive, is the hospital at the Pantocrator in Constantinople. Founded in the 12th century, it resembled a modern hospital in many respects. It had 50 to 70 beds, five wards, including for surgery and women, and an outpatient clinic. The hospital provided carefully planned meals and insisted on cleanliness and hygiene. It appears to have been used for medical education too. Another notable hospital was established at Gondishapur, Persia in the 6th century with the help of Nestorian Christians banished by Justinian. Later, there emerged highly developed and well-equipped secular hospitals in the Islamic World including ones in Bagdad and Cairo.

Byzantium and the Islamic domains facilitated the rebirth of medical knowledge in the West during the Renaissance. Damascus and Alexandria are considered to be the major conduits of knowledge from the East to the trading Italian city-states and elsewhere in the West. Medical knowledge spread in the later Middle Ages throughout Western Europe including in the universities, which became established from the 12th century onward.

Medieval Europe

Medical knowledge was lost in much of early medieval Europe outside of Byzantium and Moorish Spain and what remained of Greek and Roman knowledge was largely held by the Church. Some work in medicine occurred (e.g., by Hildegard of Bingen in the 12th century), but on the whole it was subsumed by faith, prayer, and belief in God's will. The emphasis in medicine was on care and compassion for the afflicted, consistent with Christian values, which continues to this day. We still commonly describe the health sector as healthcare in spite of today's emphasis on treatment and cure, and much of our health sector is nonprofit and affiliated with religious institutions.

Although healing in medieval Europe retained a powerful spiritual aspect, it also had a secular side in diagnosis and treatment. Herbal remedies were widely used, some from classical sources and some from the traditions of more indigenous European tribes. Many monasteries cultivated gardens of herbal treatments. In addition, surgical skills were needed for

Figure 1.7   Barber Pole in Belfast

Source: https://commons.wikimedia.org/wiki/File:Lamppost_cum_barber%27s_pole,_Belfast_-_geograph.org.uk_-_1455571.jpg

Author: Albert Bridge

Creative Commons CC 2.0

a variety of purposes including battlefield care, commonly the removal of arrows or treatment of cut wounds. The skills of barbering evolved beyond haircuts and beard trims to surgery and bloodletting; the barber's red and white pole became a symbol of the availability of such services. Red signified bloodletting services and white signified bandages. Figure 1.7 shows a modern barber pole. In the United States, the barber pole includes a blue stripe consistent with the American flag.

The Crusades, which spanned a two-century period from the late 11th century to the late 13th century proved consequential to the evolution of healthcare. When the armies from Western Europe encountered the medical expertise of the East, they inevitably adopted parts of it. They were impressed by the hospitals and skills found in Constantinople and the Byzantine Empire as well as among their Islamic foes. The Knights Templar, known for heavily armed and armored crusader knights, were an important and well-known force at that time. Another group of knights, "The Most Venerable Order of the Hospital of St. John," known as Knights Hospitaller, built their own medical facility in Jerusalem. It was large and well-run and served the stream of Western pilgrims to the Holy Land. It may also have served as a model for the development of better hospitals in Europe. Variants of the cross used for flags and shields by both the Knights Templar

Johannita lovag 13. sz. vége

Knight hospitaller late 13th century

Figure 1.8 Knight Hospitaller

Source: https://commons.wikimedia.org/wiki/File:Hospitaller_101.jpg

Author: Newbog

Creative Commons CC 2.5

and Knights Hospitaller, shown in Figure 1.8, have come to be widely used as a symbol of healthcare today. The logos for the Red Cross, Blue Cross, and Blue Shield also can be said to have these origins.

The Black Plague of the mid-14th century was a cataclysmic event in human history. The bacterium *Yersinia pestis* carried by rats and fleas devastated much of the known world, mainly via the bubonic form of plague, including Europe that had experienced substantial demographic growth over the previous two centuries. Low-income communities that had become more urbanized, densely populated, and unsanitary were especially vulnerable to this infectious pandemic. Having originated in Asia, it reached Europe from the shores of the Black Sea and killed tens and perhaps hundreds of millions of people throughout the world before it was through.

So formidable was the plague scourge, it became a weapon of war: For example, a Christian outpost known as Kaffa, now Feodosia in Crimea, was under siege by Mongols, who, in what can be called an act of biological warfare, hurled infected corpses over the walls of the city to contaminate the Christians. Besieged by this biological weaponry, they fled to Constantinople and Italy, carrying *Yersinia pestis*, as shown in Figure 1.9. Though the plague surely found its way to Europe through various other means, especially since the Mongols had opened new global trading routes, this story helps illustrate how health conditions shape history.

The plague went on to kill at least a third of Europe's population. It also stimulated an evolution from the medieval manor economy to a more modern wage-based one. In the wake of plague-induced labor shortages, serfs now sought more attractive wage-based jobs. Thus, the feudal system was undermined, as was the legitimacy of the Church. Faith in the Church was shaken by the agony of the plague and a belief that it may have been a punishment for a Church that had lost its way. Various heresies followed, eventually leading to the Protestant Reformation.

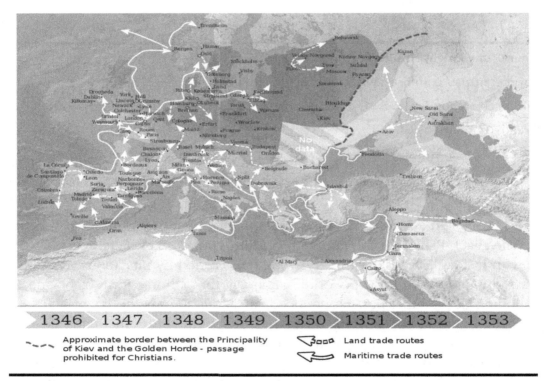

Figure 1.9 Spread of the Black Death

Source: https://commons.wikimedia.org/wiki/File:1346-1353_spread_of_the_Black_Death_in_Europe_map.svg

Author: Flappiefh

Creative Commons CC 4.0

Medicine and Healthcare in the Early Modern Period: The West

Spanning the 15th and 16th centuries, the Renaissance in Europe brought with it a renewed interest in science and the arts. Translations of Greek and Arabic texts were made not only into Latin but also into the vernacular languages of Europe. The advent of the printing press in the mid-15th century contributed to the spread of medical literature particularly through the agency of the emerging universities of Europe. Italy became a focus of Renaissance learning and the Universities of Padua and Bologna were leading centers of medical education and knowledge as were several universities outside of Italy, such as Oxford and the University of Paris, important centers dating back to the 12th century. There occurred a revitalized engagement with medical science by intellectuals and researchers. Leonardo Da Vinci, for one, advanced the understanding of the nervous system including the sense of smell and sight and provided detailed anatomical drawings, such as the one shown in Figure 1.10. As noted,

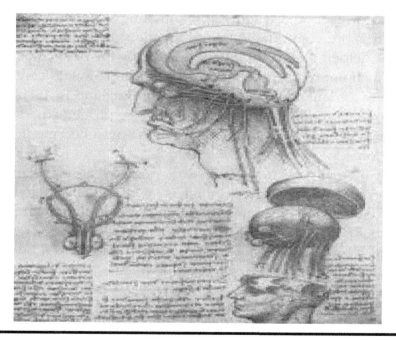

Figure 1.10   Anatomical Drawing of Leonardo Da Vinci

Source: https://commons.wikimedia.org/wiki/File:Leonardo_Da_Vinci%27s_Brain_Physiology.jpg

William Harvey became recognized for his correction of Galen's explanation of blood circulation to the more accurate pulmonary circulation we understand today.

Hospitals expanded in size, capability, and distribution during this period and became more secular and scientific. They began to shift from reliance on Church financing to other sources of revenue, including the state and local authorities. Some of these hospitals were also used for education and research. Saint Bartholomew's in London, which had been under the auspices of the Church, became a leading hospital and provided facilities for Harvey's work on the circulatory system. Generally, the shift to a more secular approach for hospitals was more pronounced in the countries that broke with the Church during the Reformation.

The evolution of hospitals from the Middle Ages to the modern era included a transition for health occupations too. As noted, the modern study of medicine evolved from the establishment of universities in the later Middle Ages, which commonly included a medical curriculum. Equally, if not more important, was the practice of medical apprenticeships in the spirit of the medieval guild. Medical and otherwise—e.g., barber-surgeons—guilds served as reservoirs of expertise. Entry to guilds was limited, however, and lengthy apprenticeships limited supply, which helped assure more comfortable livings for the skilled craftsman or physician but also helped assure some level of quality for public consumers. Such social institutions are the backdrop for occupational licensure today. Licensure, or a variant of it, was introduced in England in 1511 with the Physicians and Surgeons Act limiting the practice of medicine to those with licensure. By 1518, physicians themselves controlled medical licensure in London.

Of course, then as now, much healthcare occurred at home, and women were usually relied upon as first responders. Medical knowledge for home care was informal, often consisting of old wives' tales about herbal remedies and other panaceas passed down through the generations. Such panaceas included home treatment for burns, wounds, and broken bones. This domestic tradition facilitated women entering the medical professions in the modern era. In some cases, the wives of physicians formally or informally learned to practice medicine. As time progressed and formal education became more important, however, women found it increasingly difficult to surmount entry barriers that favored men.

Despite the rebirth of learning in the European Renaissance—its discovery of the wisdom of the ancients—there was still much ignorance about disease. At this time, for example, there was still no accepted theory of germs. There was, however, a belief held since the Middle Ages about miasmas, the spread of disease via "bad smells" carried on the air. Such was the received wisdom in both Europe and China. The theory of miasma held that pollution in the air in unclean environments could precipitate illness. To be sure, this concept does have some parallels to germ theory and could lead to effective interventions; and at the very least, it was a basis for maintaining cleanliness. It was even used to safeguard the Pope during the Black Plague: Pope Clement VI was advised by his physicians to remain within a protective ring of fire. He never did contract the plague though he was not fully compliant about remaining in the ring of fire either.

Galen had aligned himself with the theory of humors, but he also speculated that contagious diseases could be spread by "seeds." It was a notion later developed by Girolamo Fracastoro of the University of Padua in the 16th century but never became widely accepted. Interest in contagious illness was catalyzed by the spread of venereal disease in Europe. Syphilis, for example, exploded onto the scene soon after Columbus returned from the new world. It was first positively identified in 1495 in Italy among French troops besieging Naples; some of Columbus's crew were known to have gone to Italy as mercenaries and thus many believe they carried it back from the Americas. Syphilis may have quickly mutated to a more lethal form in Europe. However, it began, syphilis became a very serious disease in the Renaissance, killing millions. It was called the French Disease, Christian Disease, Spanish Pox, and other such variants until Fracastoro coined the term syphilis.

There were other frightful and more long-standing infectious diseases that plagued this period, including leprosy, bubonic plague, and smallpox. A proven theory of pathogens was not yet sufficiently developed to advise quarantine to keep infected persons isolated. Still, lepers had been isolated since at least biblical times. Ships were kept offshore for 30 days in Dubrovnik during the Black Death to help fight the infection. In fact, the term *quarantine* is of relatively recent origin, deriving from 17th century Italian and the practice of isolation to contain infection.

The introduction of syphilis to Europe possibly from the new world wrought serious devastation, but the introduction of smallpox, measles, influenza, and other pathogens to the new world brought a holocaust of epic proportions, larger than the plague in Europe. In the Americas, there was little immunity among indigenous people and they died en masse.

Mexico lost an estimated 80% of its population from 1520 to 1575 from outbreaks of smallpox and cocoliztli. Epidemiologists remain uncertain about exactly what cocoliztli was, but recent studies indicate salmonella was partly responsible for it. Severe drought is thought to have played a role as well. Indigenous people in eastern North America were similarly devastated by diseases in the 16th and 17th centuries, which greatly facilitated English and French colonization. Disease followed them westward among native Americans, with major depopulations in the 18th and 19th centuries. Cholera arrived somewhat later than other pathogens. Associated with dirty, fecal-contaminated water, it first arrived in Europe from India in the 19th century and soon found its way to the Americas with deadly consequences.

India and China

This chapter ends with some discussion of the medical traditions of India and China, which evolved largely independent of the West until the early modern period. Indian medical knowledge did mix with Persian and Arab learning over the centuries, but the Indian tradition is often considered mostly a separate evolution. Existing writings on Indian medicine date well into antiquity. *Ayurveda* details medical learning and oral traditions that date back perhaps 8,000 years. It includes the use of medications commonly derived from herbs and other plants as well as surgical interventions. Not surprisingly, there was a strong spiritual dimension to Indian medicine and theoretical concepts of balance that were important, analogous to humorism in the West. Meditation, stress reduction, and massage were also central to healing in this tradition. Ayurvedic medicine, the basis of traditional healthcare in India and the broader subcontinent, has many adherents and is an integral part of healthcare alongside Western medicine.

Chinese history is shrouded in mystery prior to the Shang dynasty of the second millennium BC. Evidence of very early medical knowledge must be gleaned from tools and records etched in bones. We do know of the use of herbal medicines from this period and a written record from the first millennium BC helps to inform us of these practices. A medical text known as the *Yellow Emperor's Canon of Internal Medicine* is commonly dated to the 3rd century BC. It is thought to have been compiled over previous centuries and is foundational to the Chinese medical tradition. Chinese traditional medicine developed over the centuries to provide thousands of panaceas, and like remedies in the West and India, it relies on notions of balance, in China known as yin and yang. Theories of anatomical meridians that transmit life energy and acupuncture feature prominently in Chinese medicine as do theories of cold temperatures and bodily damage. Sanitation and public health works were established in ancient China, evident, for example, in sophisticated water and sewage systems. Toilets were most commonly simple holes in the ground with two flat stones or bricks to stand on while squatting and the resulting "night soil" was carried away to be used as fertilizer.

Western medicine was introduced to China in the age of Western exploration, but mostly in the 19th century. It gained prominence, especially in more urban and coastal regions. At the time of the Communist ascendency in 1949, access to western medicine remained limited. The party leadership recognized its important role, and while Mao Tse Tung might not have been a devoted adherent to traditional Chinese medicine, he recognized its deep-seated place in China's health sector. Consequently, he supported a dual healthcare system with elements of both traditional and Western scientific medicine. Today, China has both traditional and Western hospitals and consumers have a choice of which tradition to follow. Figure 1.11 shows a mixing of traditional remedies at a Nanjing hospital. When the Nobel Prize was awarded to Tu Youyou in 2015 for work with artemisinin, traditional Chinese

Figure 1.11 Traditional Chinese Medicine

Source: https://commons.wikimedia.org/wiki/File:Apothecary_mixing_traditional_chinese_medicin_(%E4%B8%AD%E8%8D%AF%E6%88%BF)_at_Jiangsu_Chinese_Medical_Hospital_in_Nanjing_%E5%8D%97%E4%BA%AC,_China_(34326619184).jpg

Author: Kristoffer Trolle

Creative Commons CC 2.0

medicine was given a boost: Artemisinin, derived from a Chinese plant, has been used to treat malaria for thousands of years.

Conclusion

This chapter provides a brisk tour of the evolution of healthcare from Neolithic times to the modern era. It shows the influence of the ancients and European practitioners of the Middle Ages as well as the Islamic contributions to that story. The stream of history has flowed in currents, mingling those contributions. The traditions of India and China, largely unknown to the West until recently, are now part of the globalized flow of healthcare development. We have seen that the impact of spiritual and religious institutions from ancient Egypt to medieval Europe and beyond has been an important theme, but nothing has been as powerful as the expansion of scientific knowledge. Biomedical understanding in its infancy, while impressive in places and times in the past, does not remotely compare with the present. Those born today will experience a wealth of new technologies that will extend and enhance their lives. The potential before us is awe-inspiring. The health sector looms large in our economy and prosperity has never been so entwined with its evolution. How this may unfold is a central question for this book.

Chapter 2

Early Evolution of American Healthcare

Introduction

It has become routine among many Americans to complain that our healthcare system is in crisis because it costs far too much. In 2021, for example, the cost of health insurance for a family of four exceeded $22,000, and it continues to rise, with no end in sight, driven largely by expensive new technologies and generous health insurance. How did we arrive at this unsustainable condition of skyrocketing costs, the crisis in which we find ourselves at present? The answer is multifold and perhaps the best way to understand it begins by reviewing the historical record, which, along with the outlook for healthcare and the US economy going forward, is much the purpose of this book: to show how we evolved to our current state of affairs and the choices at hand for addressing the present crises. To that end, this and the following chapters trace the history of American healthcare from its origin to the present. Before exploring that record, however, it is necessary to identify some prominent features of our contemporary healthcare crisis.

Why Healthcare Costs So Much

A myriad of reasons, including public policies, have brought us to the way we experience healthcare in America today. They include the origin and development of health insurance, market power and the nature of

DOI: 10.4324/9781003186137-3

competition in healthcare, information asymmetries, licensure of providers and our deference to them, and the lack of sufficient mechanisms to prevent allocation of resources to the health sector when costs do not justify benefits.

Health insurance: Tax-free health insurance over time encouraged the spread and reach of health insurance, which in turn encouraged competition in the health sector not on price, but rather perceived quality. For most health expenditures, there is little need to be concerned with the price tag when others pick up the bill. The use of new technology is a primary means of improving at least the perception of quality and new technology is the leading cause of cost escalation over the long run. A medical arms race has brought many important innovations but also high prices, especially for private payers.

To be sure, insurance makes sense to protect wealth in the face of uncertain, but potentially catastrophic health expenditures. This is the case for many risks such as fire, automobile accidents, and professional liability where individuals averse to large financial loss pool risk. But health insurance is a double-edged sword bolstering efficiency by protecting risk-averse beneficiaries but undermining efficiency by promoting overconsumption when consumers do not face the full cost of production. Health consumption is less random, and consumers are more likely to overconsume than for other insured sectors of the economy.

Market Power: Healthcare markets rarely are characterized by competitive conditions. Buyers and sellers commonly have at least some monopoly power, and output is seldom commodity like. Producers command brand loyalty and differentiate to bolster their market power. Competition often focuses on signaling quality rather than price.

Information asymmetries: Another perspective, and one foundational to health economics, addresses the way the health sector deals with information asymmetries. Information asymmetries refer to the problem of imbalance in the information held by buyers and sellers. The problem is not unique to healthcare but is particularly acute here. For example, well-trained physicians, dentists, and others possess much more health-related information than the typical consumer. The consuming public relies on them as agents to advance their health. But this can lead to abuse when providers induce unnecessary or costly services that do not have commensurate benefits. So, American society has evolved high levels of deference toward providers, not-for-profit organizational status including affiliations with religious and other well-meaning organizations to help assure the consuming public that they can trust their providers. These arrangements provide a degree of comfort to the consuming public, but they have not prevented high levels of inefficiency.

Licensure: Other public policies have undermined efficient competition in healthcare too. Notably, occupational licensure restricts the supply of healthcare providers and thereby drives up prices. Many economists are concerned that occupational licensure protects professions from competition more than consumers from low quality.

Allocation of Resources to Health: Societies around the world value human life and find it difficult to draw the line and identify when healthcare spending is excessive. How much health spending is too much? How much is a life worth and when should resources be allocated elsewhere even if it means people may die? The COVID-19 epidemic brought such issues into the spotlight with agonizing and conflicting policies regarding the right balance between saving lives and livelihoods.

Economists commonly look to the institutional arrangements of healthcare to understand why we are in this predicament of soaring healthcare costs and they offer different theories that address this question. Perhaps, the most prominent has to do with the economic gain in the health sector that evolved to accommodate providers and other healthcare interests. Costs in the United States are driven primarily by high prices, and these high prices are supported by a myriad of institutional arrangements. Health professions, notably, are protected from competition by institutions that evolved in their favor via practices such as third-party insurance, tax-free insurance, occupational licensure, a lack of price transparency, and a high level of deference to providers by the consuming public.

This evolutionary outcome and overallocation of resources to the health sector have worked well for providers. They are among the most prosperous Americans, and many economists believe pay is excessive for many health occupations. This is the case when compensation exceeds the amount necessary to attract and retain people in these fields. Economists refer to this excess as economic rent. The pursuit of windfall economic gains is called rent-seeking. It is no surprise that health careers are a top choice among college students today. Perhaps, the intellectual rewards of the academic content and the gratification of caregiving are important reasons as well, but many economists suspect rent-seeking; they also predict that applicants to such programs would greatly diminish if financial returns were to decline.

The late Princeton Economist Uwe Reinhardt argued that these and other problems in American healthcare have simply "priced out" the American public. It is clear something must give, but it is not clear what that is. This cannot continue indefinitely. Solutions will evolve but if the past provides guidance the path may be tortuous. Winston Churchill is sometimes credited with arguing "Americans Will Always Do the Right Thing—After Exhausting All the Alternatives." Let us hope this will not be the case here. How did we get to the present crisis of unsustainable healthcare spending? The journey, as we shall see, has been a long and winding one.

Early American Healthcare: 17th and 18th Centuries

Healthcare in 17th-century colonial America was characterized by general informality, in which apothecaries (pharmacists) and physicians relied on apprenticeships for much of their training. There was no wall between the two and pharmacists could freely diagnose and treat illnesses as well as dispense medicines. Physicians also provided all three services. Insurance or third-party payment was rare, and households commonly paid out-of-pocket for healthcare services to providers outside the family. The in-kind payment was common, too, as families would pay with their own farm or household products.

Formal training for medical practitioners was limited. The first medical school in colonial America was established in 1765 in Philadelphia at the University of Pennsylvania. Columbia University followed with a medical school in New York in 1767 and then Harvard in Boston in 1782. Formal medical education was not seen as necessary in an age where medical knowledge was far less advanced.

Colonial providers were usually unschooled, at least formally, unless they had training in England or elsewhere. And even if they did have a degree, those qualifications were limited by the very incomplete level of science known at the time in areas such as anatomy, physiology, and surgery. Much of the formal curriculum relied on knowledge of classical medicine augmented by some medieval additions and a few modern advances. The ancient system of humoral medicine with its emphasis on balance remained in vogue in the colonial period and beyond. As noted in Chapter 1, George Washington died in 1799 when his physicians and caregivers believed bloodletting to be the appropriate treatment for a bad sore throat. He was bled multiple times and administered an enema to restore balance. This treatment did not work out well.

There were concepts akin to germ theory that had existed for centuries, such as miasma, which postulated that unhealthy fog or air could cause disease. Germ theory did not become conventional wisdom until the late 19th century in spite of the identification of bacteria in the 17th century with the advent of the microscope. Although many practitioners of healthcare did believe in cleanliness to promote health, and modern nursing emphasized it, conditions were often dismally unsanitary.

Vaccination against diseases was limited to smallpox until the end of the 19th century. Smallpox vaccination is traced back to at least 16th-century China when people were inoculated against the disease by having them inhale pulverized smallpox scabs. Vaccination for smallpox in the United States first occurred in the late 18th century, following the work of Edward Jenner, albeit without a full understanding of how the protection worked.

In the 19th century, there was a heavy reliance on household remedies; women wore multiple hats providing various services including that of healthcare provider dispensing treatments handed down from generation to generation; mothers, grandmothers, and neighbors were relied upon in the colonial period and beyond to provide this home care. Unfortunately, women who aspired for a career in medicine were generally barred from apprenticeships and later found difficulty in getting medical school admission. Elizabeth Blackwell was the first American woman admitted to a medical school in 1847 in New York State, but a balance between male and female medical students was not achieved until recent times.

Those who were literate in British North America in the 18th century may have had access to books and other printed matter. The first American medical journal did not appear until 1790 with *Medical Papers published by the Massachusetts Medical Society*. But books and other publications were available: some 200 were published before 1785 mostly in Philadelphia, Boston, and New York. The renowned Benjamin Rush contributed including *Sermons to Gentleman upon Temperance and Exercise* in 1772. One notable book was the *First Lines of the Practice of Physic* by William Cullen, first appearing in Scotland but later republished multiple times in America. Other books, more widely used by laymen, included *Every Man His Own Doctor* published around 1727 by John Tennent, a Virginia physician, and later in the early 1780s, *The Medical Pocketbook: for Those Who Are, and for All Who Wish to Be, Physicians* by John Elliott. There were other sources that focused on medications, many of which were natural remedies. An example is John Tweedy's, *A Catalogue of Druggs and Chymical and Galenical Medicines* appearing in 1760.

And lest we forget, not all of colonial America was British. There was a long-standing settlement by the Spanish in Santa Fe, which dated to the time

of Cervantes in the early 17th century. By 1626, there was already resistance
to regulation imposed by the Crown as residents of Santa Fe objected to
exclusion of nonlicensed physicians, even in North America, so distant from
the mother country. Medical care in Spanish territory relied on the technical
expertise of medicine in Spain, such as it was, among its universities, and
physicians. Spain too adhered to the ancient traditions of humoral medicine. But unlike English colonies, the Catholic Church had a much greater
influence and maintained traditions established in the early Middle Ages.
Healthcare both spiritual and physical, continued to be an important part of
the Church mission, and this was brought to the new world. Medical technology was not limited to the received wisdom of Europe as practices of
indigenous people were integrated with the western approaches. In addition,
as in other parts of North America, women and households administered
much of the necessary healthcare. Books were limited, but the mission in
Santa Barbara, California, housed an impressive collection that included
health-related holdings. A quick perusal of the current library holdings finds
that the oldest includes the work of Pedanius Dioscorides, a noted and
widely read Greek physician of the 1st century AD who served the Roman
military and the Badianus manuscript from 1552 detailing Aztec herbal remedies. More recent writings from the 17th and 18th centuries detail diagnostics and treatments including medications. One author, a Spanish Cistercian
monk of the 18th century named Antonio Jose Rodriquez, integrated the
secular and spiritual in medical and Church thought.

The 19th Century: Economic Growth and Transition to Modern American Healthcare

A public health approach to understanding the evolution of health is important. This has been known since at least the time of ancient Babylonia and
the Romans, who built impressive public works. Sanitation, or lack of it,
explains a great deal of mortality over the ages. But, perhaps, at no time
was improvement in public health more consequential in the United States
than in the 19th century. Levels of sanitation improved dramatically in urban
environments.

Beyond sanitation and environmental conditions more generally, economic conditions advanced in 19th-century America. Studies consistently
show that the standard of living is a primary determinant of health in part
because of better access to healthcare, but for other reasons as well. Per
capita income, when statistically adjusted to filter out other factors, such as

education, race, or age, is a very important determinant of health for reasons not fully understood. Wherever and whenever one looks at disparities in health, the level and distribution of income and wealth play a major role and the standard of living advanced in this time period, particularly in the later 19th century.

Studies of the determinants of health also show the importance of social factors, especially education. Levels of education advanced in this period, helping people better understand how to prevent illness and provide treatment when necessary. Education may also be a proxy for how much people are willing to invest in the future even if it entails sacrifice in the present. Those who invest in education for the long run arguably also behave in ways that promote health in the long run. This long-run orientation helps explain why health and education are correlated.

Economic Backdrop to 19th-Century America

The level of prosperity, at least as measured by per capita income, depends on productivity. Economists focus on labor productivity, output per worker, which in the long run corresponds to inflation-adjusted wages. For millennia, labor productivity gains and the standard of living were constrained by agricultural technologies in the domestication of animals and plants. These were developed in the Neolithic Revolution that commenced about 12,000 years ago. It ultimately transitioned our species away from hunter-gatherer lifestyles. The predominant view is that this was an improvement and paved the way for civilization. It surely led to more output and a good standard of living for a portion of the population. But some argue the gains of the agricultural revolution led primarily to greater population and a Malthusian trap, with large numbers of impoverished people persisting for millennia. And new diseases, such as smallpox and tuberculosis, emerged stemming from interactions with animals among those engaged in animal husbandry. It can be argued that Pre-Neolithic hunter–gatherers may have had better lives.

Everything changed with the Industrial Revolution. Economic historians usually place the beginning of the Industrial Revolution in the United Kingdom, especially England, in the mid to late 18th century. There, the advent of steam power fueled by coal was a critical dimension. Steam-driven pumps were employed to drain the coal mines when water intruded. Steam power was used to drive mechanization in the textile industry and was then used in the transport sector with the introduction of steamships and railroads.

The Napoleonic Wars catalyzed the development of industry in the United States. The trade embargo established by President Jefferson in December 1807 to avoid war (with limited success since the United States was drawn into the War of 1812 anyway) greatly reduced the shipment of cotton and other products to England and elsewhere. But the boycott of imports from abroad protected American manufacturers and provided the opportunity to greatly expand domestic industry. Much of this was in the Northeast and later the Midwest, where nascent American industry capitalized on new technologies to drive the takeoff of the American economy. Increased output per worker led to a sustained rise in wages. (California, which entered the union after the Mexican War and during the Gold Rush in 1850, was afforded a large degree of geographical protection.) The railroad did not span the nation, coast to coast, until 1869 providing a window of time for the indigenous industry to develop without much competition.

After the Civil War, a new generation of technologies, including low-cost Bessemer steel production, telegraph and then telephone communications, electrical power, and an expanding chemical industry further fueled growth and prosperity. Steel rails soon replaced iron ones, and steel was used to replace antiquated wooden ships in the Navy and elsewhere. Steel facilitated the construction of high-rise buildings and bridges. However, other technologies were also important, including paper production and the evolution of machine tools. The development of fertilizers in the 19th century improved agricultural productivity along with steam and later internal combustion engine equipment. But the improvement did not end there. Central heating and ready access to electricity improved living conditions for much of urban America by the end of the 19th century. Robert Gordon of Northwestern University argues there was an unprecedented, and unlikely to be repeated, improvement in the standard of living associated with urbanization that is only partially revealed by the rising per capita income. He asserts that the pace of improvement that began after the Civil War and extended through the middle of the 20th century has given way to more modest gains in living standards that will persist.

Healthcare Advances

The latter part of the 19th century experienced a remarkable transformation and improvement in social welfare in American cities. Improvement in public health reduced mortality and extended life expectancy. Life expectancy in Massachusetts at birth (whites only) increased from 39 in 1850 to 48 in 1900. Systematic approaches to sanitation including food- and waterborne diseases, vaccination, and quarantine measures helped curb infectious diseases. An abundance of food supplied by an improving railroad network and other forms of transportation was critical. But life improved in other important ways. Higher incomes and a higher standard of living advanced more and more of the population toward high mass consumption. The quality of life, at least in urban areas, where homes and apartments were connected to electricity, a sewage system, clean water, telephones, heating, and iceboxes with a readily available supply of ice provided a major advance in the standard of living for increasing numbers and percentages of Americans. Figure 2.1 shows how income grew rapidly after the Civil War and into the 21st century.

Better public health and higher incomes were the primary drivers of improved health as the 19th century progressed. Medical care was a secondary but important source of general health improvement. Hospitals began a transition from philanthropically supported institutions focused on providing

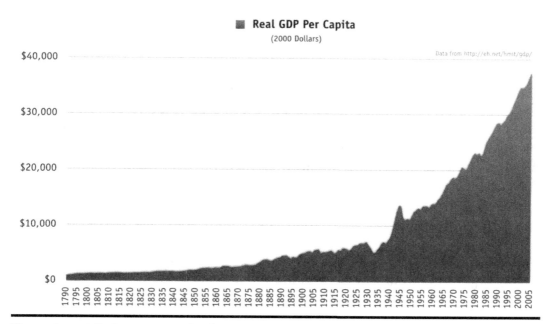

Figure 2.1   US GDP per Capita from 1790 to 2005

Source: https://en.wikipedia.org/wiki/File:Real_gdp_per_capita.png

Creative Commons CC 3.0 (GNU)

care to the sick, infirm, and dying to their present form. They were often affiliated with religious organizations; communities supported their hospitals as a matter of civic pride and generally did not make money. This began to change in the latter part of the century. Hospitals could increasingly offer good outcomes as medical technologies developed and hospitals commenced a transition from charity to paying beds. The nature of hospitals changed, evolving to become the physician's workshop where necessary infrastructure for patient treatment and care was housed. By the end of the century, hospitals provided diagnostic equipment such as X-ray machines, surgical equipment and supplies as well as laboratories for analysis. Little of this could be readily stored in the physician's travel bag. Physicians still made house calls but as the century wore on, the option of hospitalization for follow-up became more and more common and necessary.

To illustrate the changes that occurred in healthcare, especially in the latter half of the century, consider the cases of Presidents Garfield and Cleveland. President Garfield was shot by a deranged man on July 2, 1881. He was gravely wounded but did not die immediately when shot. He was cared for by a team of physicians who did not subscribe to the new germ theory of infection and did not sterilize when probing Garfield's body to recover a bullet. They repeatedly probed for a bullet lodged in Garfield's abdomen with unsterilized fingers. To make matters worse, they misjudged the trajectory of the bullet leading to multiple efforts at recovery. Garfield eventually developed infections that are thought by most to have ultimately killed him. He died on September 19, 1881. Many believe Garfield's death was avoidable had his physicians maintained better levels of cleanliness. A mere 12 years later, Grover Cleveland was found to have a rapidly growing cancer in the roof of his mouth. He received surgery (on a yacht) with nitrous oxide and ether as anesthetics and antiseptically sterilized instruments. Physicians removed five teeth and his upper left palate and jawbone, and he was soon back at home and fitted with prosthetics. Nothing was visible to the public. Though stories of the surgery leaked, Cleveland denied the reports. The two stories are quite a contrast in late 19th century medicine and instructive to the extent of change that occurred in the final decades of the century.

Imaging technology was an important new development at the end of the 19th century. X-ray machines were available for injured troops in the Spanish-American War in 1898. The machines aboard the hospital ship *Relief*, as shown in Figure 2.2, as well as the *Missouri* and *Bay State* which were anchored offshore in Cuba, were particularly helpful in pinpointing the location of bullets embedded in wounded soldiers.

Figure 2.2 X-ray on the USS Relief

Source: File: https://commons.wikimedia.org/wiki/File:USS_Relief_(1896)_X-ray.jpg
Public Domain

Improving Health in the 19th Century

Population pressure and urban opportunities drove large numbers of people to rapidly growing cities of this industrializing era. The shift toward cities is shown in Figure 2.3. Unfortunately, early 19th-century cities were abysmally lacking in sanitation awareness by the standards of today. Fetid water was everywhere, and sewage systems were only introduced in the latter half of the century. In addition, there was little emphasis on safe working conditions, and many factories were plagued by industrial accidents.

Health often deteriorated for those workers leaving the farm for the city in the mid-19th century. Note Figure 2.4. It shows a decline in life expectancy at age 10 as urbanization accelerated. Life expectancy only begins to increase consistently at the end of the century with the advent of public health measures and improved nutrition. Adult height mirrored the trend in life expectancy, having declined significantly between the middle and end of the century.

The introduction of sewer systems and widespread provision of clean water in the latter part of the 19th century was central to reducing the mortality and morbidity associated with cholera, dysentery, and typhoid, among other diseases. This set the stage for impressive health gains in the

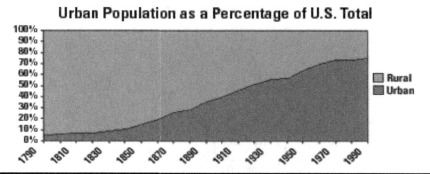

Figure 2.3   Urban Population as a Percentage of US Total

Source: https://pubs.usgs.gov/circ/2004/circ1252/fig.2.gif

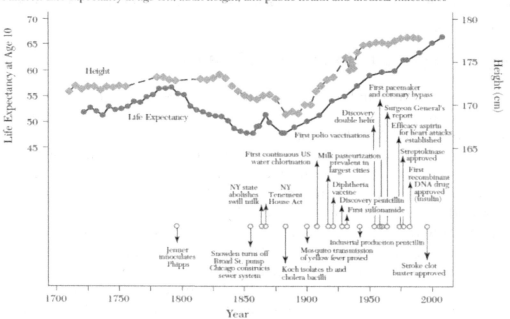

Figure 2.4   Technological Advance and Health

Source: Costa, Dora L. "Health and the Economy in the United States from 1750 to the Present." *Journal of Economic Literature* 53, no. 3 (2015): 503–70.

Reprinted with permission of the Journal of Economic Literature.

20th century. There were massive infrastructure programs in American cities in the later 19th century, establishing municipal systems of sanitation and clean water. The movement was facilitated by the Great Stink of London in 1858. A rapidly expanding London dumped human waste into the Thames and by the summer of 1858, the stench had become unbearable. A city-wide system of sewers was constructed over the following decades, which much improved both health and environmental quality. Parallel developments occurred in American cities including Chicago and New York. Chemical treatment of sewage and water systems, including the use of chlorine, was introduced by the end of the century. The use of fluoride in water systems to prevent tooth decay came later in the 20th century. But implementation is inconsistent as many communities opt to forgo this public health measure.

Industrialization also led to hazardous air pollution. Again, England was the first to experience serious problems. Coal fueled the first few waves of industrialization and with the burning of coal came copious amounts of atmospheric effluent. London was among the worst. Suspended particulate matter increased steadily throughout the 18th and most of the 19th centuries. Legislation in 1891 to curb the worst offenders and a shift toward more suburban and less dense residential patterns contributed to a decline in severity. Increasing use of gas for cooking and other purposes also helped. Nevertheless, coal and industrial air pollution remained elevated in the urban environments of the United Kingdom, the United States, and elsewhere. Respiratory ailments including bronchitis, tuberculosis, and lung cancer were problematic.

Health Technology and Education

The 19th century was marked by the unprecedented advance in health-related knowledge and technology. Most important was the discovery and widespread acceptance of germ theory. Generally credited to Louis Pasteur and Joseph Lister, the discovery of bacteria's role in disease was transformational. Robert Koch, a German microbiologist and medical researcher, identified the bacteria causing anthrax, tuberculosis, and cholera. More broadly, he was important in developing the science to isolate and identify pathogens causing many diseases. The development of vaccines was catalyzed by advances in the theory of germs.

The theory of germs set the stage for the use of antiseptics beginning with carbolic acid and the recognition that cleanliness and sanitation were of the utmost importance in health maintenance. Modern vaccines for cholera were launched first in 1885, and by the end of the century vaccines were found for anthrax, rabies, typhoid, diphtheria, and bubonic plague. The combination of public health measures and vaccines effectively combated many deadly infections. The consensus is that public health measures were commonly more effective than vaccines. They often preceded vaccines and infection rates greatly subsided by the time many vaccines arrived.

Other important technologies also emerged in the 19th century. They include the stethoscope, introduced in 1816, which amplified the sounds of the heart and breathing. Human blood transfusions were pioneered by James Blundell in England reportedly in 1818. The ophthalmoscope came along in the 1840s and 1850s to greatly assist the diagnosis of eye health. The use of anesthetics in surgery, beginning with ether in the 1840s, enabled a new era in surgical possibility and far less pain for the patient. Successful human heart surgery occurred toward the end of the century, and the X-ray machine was introduced by Wilhelm Rontgen in 1895.

This new, more technologically advanced world called for higher levels of education. Medical education and health profession education evolved accordingly in the 19th century. A new and better understanding of anatomy and physiology was attained following rapid developments in biology and biochemistry. Some medical schools embraced a scientific approach and incorporated the latest technology, while others adhered to paradigms of alternative medicine; increasingly in this period, alternative approaches were viewed with skepticism by adherents of the medical orthodoxy and were seen by some as outright quackery. Concerns about the quality of medical education reached a watershed in the early 20th century when most medical schools were shut down because they lacked the scientific rigor expected by medical elites. Allopathic medical schools, those that focus on symptoms and treatment using scientific approaches, are the only ones now permitted to award the MD, a qualification accepted for licensure throughout the United States.

The exception to allopathic medicine that survived the scientific transformation of medical education is osteopathic medicine, associated with the DO degree, and is accepted for licensure in all 50 states. Osteopathic medicine and other forms of alternative medicine, such as homeopathy, take a more holistic approach to healthcare at least in theory. Osteopathic care relies in part on manipulative medicine which focuses on the manipulation of skeletal joints and adjacent tissues, but in large part it follows the allopathic regime. The first osteopathic medical school was established by AT Still in 1892 in Kirksville Missouri.

Nursing education also evolved in this period. Florence Nightingale, regarded as the founder of modern nursing, was widely recognized for her groundbreaking work in the Crimean War during the 1850s caring for wounded British soldiers. She later established a professional school of nursing in London in the 1860s. Her work pioneered improvement in sanitation and cleanliness as well as statistical and empirical approaches to analyze and communicate healthcare issues. In many respects, Nightingale's counterpart in the United States was Clara Barton. Active in caring for the wounded during the Civil War, Barton often risked her own life on the front lines. She later established the American Red Cross and served as its senior executive from 1881 to 1904. The first professional nursing schools in the United States appeared in 1873, in New York, and were soon followed by schools in New Haven and Boston, employing the Nightingale model and relying heavily on apprenticeships and exposure to clinical environments. Nursing schools rapidly proliferated relying increasingly on theoretical and didactic courses, which displaced some apprenticeship training.

Dental and pharmacy education also were shaped by the scientific advances of the 19th century. Formal schools of dentistry were slow to evolve, as most dentists were trained by apprenticeship, but new technologies helped underpin the need for formal dental education. The advent of anesthetics such as nitrous oxide and ether in the 1840s was of great importance, particularly for dental extractions. Later, the foot-driven drill was introduced in 1871. Thirteen schools of dentistry had been established between 1840 and 1868, but the total number of graduates was only 1,065 by 1869. The schools were located primarily in the Northeast and Midwest, although one was established in New Orleans in 1867. New schools continued to be formed for the remainder of the century and were distributed more broadly throughout the country.

Formal dental education was slowed by the low esteem dentistry held among physicians and medical educators, who were unwilling to integrate dental and medical education. As a result, dental education evolved independently in the United States. But it adhered to the same pattern of education as other health professions with heavy reliance on apprenticeships, yielding over time to more didactic and theoretical classroom training. Licensure for dentistry at the state level first occurred after the Civil War and later spread throughout the country.

The transition from apothecary to pharmacist in the United States largely occurred in the 19th century. Pharmacy became more professionalized. Schools of Pharmacy first appeared in Philadelphia and New York in the

1820s and proliferated thereafter. Licensure was first introduced in New Orleans in 1769 by Spanish authorities and regulation and oversight accelerated in the 19th century. The establishment of the American Pharmacists Association in 1852 further served to professionalize pharmacists and measures that followed helped differentiate pharmacists from "snake oil" salesmen. New medications often chemically derived from known natural substances fueled demand for qualified professionals. Morphine derived from opium poppies was introduced at the beginning of the century. Quinine, a malaria medicine derived from quina-quina bark, used by native Americans and brought to Europe by the Spanish, was introduced in 1820. Paracetamol, also known as acetaminophen, the active ingredient of Tylenol, was developed and identified as a pain reliever in the 1890s. Aspirin, derived from the willow, a folk medicine for millennia, was commercially introduced by Bayer in 1899.

Healthcare Finance

Payment for health services in the 19th century was largely out-of-pocket or provided as charity. Some organizations such as the military provided care to members, but for the most part, households provided their own care, or paid for it directly. Hospitalization costs were often beyond the means of a typical household, and they were financed by religious, community, or other philanthropic organizations. For most Americans, the primary financial threat of illness was not the cost of care but rather lost productivity and wages.

The social impact of lost wages became more pronounced as the United States industrialized. This was also the case in Europe, and it was there that institutions first developed to finance costs of illness. Social turmoil threatened the existing order and recognizing this, Otto von Bismarck, Chancellor of a newly united Germany, established sickness funds for various classes of workers. These expanded to become more inclusive over time. Many regard this as the foundation of modern health insurance, but it should be pointed out that the focus was on replacing lost wages, not medical bills; it was more akin to what Americans know as sick leave. Today, sickness funds in Germany are the primary payors of medical costs.

The United States did not legislate health insurance, as did Europe, until the 20th century. But the private pooling of funds for sick leave and medical costs in the latter part of the century did occur; they were called industrial sickness funds, first emerging in the Civil War era and proliferated thereafter.

Industrial sickness funds could be organized and managed by firms, unions, or other organizations. Fraternal organizations were important providers of sickness funds and these included groups such as the Masonic Order, Elks, and Odd Fellows. The federal government identified 1,259 sickness funds in the census of 1890. They were quite widespread, especially in the Northeast, Midwest, California, Texas, and Louisiana. Workers typically contributed a percentage, perhaps 1% of their wages, that was pooled to provide health-related benefits. American progressives in the late 19th century sought publicly provided health insurance and began a political movement to create and expand benefits that persist today.

Chapter 3

20th- and 21st-Century Evolution of American Healthcare

The 20th Century Professionalization of Health Occupations

The early 20th century was a period of rapid evolution in the health sector, so much so it is regarded as a watershed in the professionalization of healthcare. Of greatest note perhaps was the work of Abraham Flexner, whose book *The American College: A Criticism*, published in 1908, came to the attention of the Carnegie Foundation. He was soon after selected by the foundation to lead a study of medical education, although he had no medical training himself. The Flexner Report, published in 1910, concluded that American medical education was not consistently up to the standards required for the 20th century. Some medical schools were found to be solid, and Johns Hopkins University was held to be exemplary. But Flexner concluded there was insufficient scientific or empirical rigor in most medical programs. The report, calling for more rigorous admission criteria as well as more clinical training, was embraced by much of the medical establishment and the public at large. State regulation of the profession catalyzed change. Medical licensure soon required graduation from an accredited program, and accreditation criteria largely conformed to Flexner's recommendations. In its wake, the Flexner Report's call for heightened standards led to the closure of most medical schools in the United States, hitting rural and Black institutions especially hard. Many of the medical schools that survived were subject to major dislocation in curriculum, admissions, and other facets of the education program. This occurred at a time when demand for medical services was rising, in part because of new technology, diagnostics, and procedures, but also because of rising incomes. The combination of sharply reduced physician supply and increasing demand elevated physician income that persists to this day.

The professionalization of education in the health professions extended to other occupations with more rigorous training required for dentistry, pharmacy, and nursing to name a few. Among them, healthcare management was increasingly recognized as a new and important field. Hospital administrators had historically come from the ranks of nuns and others not formally trained in management. The first and short-lived undergraduate program in healthcare management was launched at Marquette University in Milwaukee in the 1920s. More sustained and influential programs were established at the graduate level. The topic of healthcare management was of interest to the Rockefeller Foundation, which supported Michael Davis, a Columbia University–trained economist and sociologist interested in professionalizing the occupation. Davis was uncertain about the most appropriate setting for health management education and was torn between business and medical schools. He believed traditional management disciplines such as accounting, finance, and economics were essential. But he also saw great value in immersion in the production and culture of health services, which healthcare settings could provide. Ultimately, he called for a fusion of the two. The tension, evident then, exists to the present day, with no clear locus for academic healthcare management.

Davis later founded a master's program in hospital and healthcare management at the University of Chicago in 1934, integrating business and health science exposure. A similar program was established at Northwestern University in the early 1940s. Owing in part to these early programs, the center of gravity in the mid-20th century for healthcare management was Chicago, and it persists to this day. The headquarters for the American Hospital Association, the American College of Healthcare Executives, and the American Medical Association are in Chicago, even as the study of healthcare management has diffused throughout the country.[1]

Public health had emerged as a separate community of inquiry by the early 20th century. The focus on population health as well as social and environmental determinates of health, as opposed to patient-centric disease, was a key reason for the rift with academic medicine. Separate schools were thought to better protect the different orientations of academic public health from the larger and increasingly affluent medical community. As a result, new schools of public health were established at Tulane in 1912, Yale in 1915, and Johns Hopkins in 1916. Others followed based on the Johns Hopkins model at Harvard and Columbia. Public health evolved as a separate area of academic inquiry divided into epidemiology, community health, environmental and occupational health, biostatistics, and healthcare management.

The Spanish Flu

The Spanish flu broke out in 1918 killing millions worldwide, including at least 500,000 in the United States. The cause of the pandemic was not clear at the time as virology was only in its infancy. There were successive waves between 1918 and 1920 across the globe, and wartime conditions in Europe were thought to have amplified the spread and severity. Censorship during the war prevented reporting of circumstances in many countries but the epidemic spread to neutral Spain, which did not have such censorship, and with widespread coverage there, the epidemic became known as the Spanish flu. Mortality was particularly high among young adults who often experienced a damaging heightened immune response called cytokine storms. Americans responded in much the same way during the COVID pandemic a century later, following the same protocols of social distancing and masks. Figure 3.1 shows a makeshift hospital ward at Camp Funston, Kansas, where the

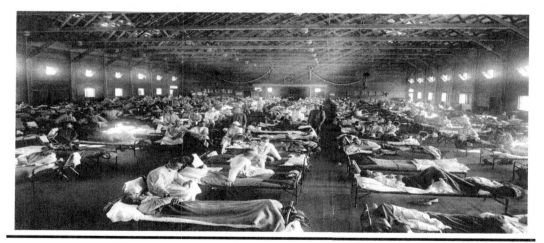

Figure 3.1 Spanish Flu Treatment in Kansas, 1918

Source: www.rawpixel.com/image/2298586/free-photo-image-spanish-flu-pandemic-covid

Public Domain

disease is first known to have appeared in the United States. Certainly, from a contemporary perspective, it is regrettable that much of what was learned during the Spanish flu did not become a mainstay of public health education. Perhaps now, after COVID, pandemic preparedness and policy will gain more prominence in healthcare curricula and policy planning.

Committee on the Costs of Medical Care

The shift from charitable to paying beds continued apace in the early 20th century and with it the rapid expansion of hospitals and hospital capacity. It became clear that the health sector was becoming a very important and technology-based part of the economy. As it turned out, the hospital evolved to become indispensable to the practice of medicine, at least for many of the specialties. This evolution was not easy, undergoing trial and error to find the best institutional arrangements. At the same time, there was corresponding concern about the rising costs of healthcare. The shortage of physicians was one factor in this rise, but the complexity of the health sector and associated costs were also becoming apparent. To address those issues, the Committee on the Costs of Medical Care (CCMC) was formed in 1926, partly in response to a call for research into healthcare costs by President Coolidge. Supported by foundations, the CCMC operated from 1927 to 1932. The mission of the committee was to study the economic organization of medical care. At the time, the health sector was lagging in the transition toward large-scale corporate forms of organization. President Herbert Hoover (formerly Secretary of Commerce) was familiar with the committee's work and was a staunch advocate for modern forms of business organization that could reap economies of scale. Clearly, the rapid expansion of hospitals called for new forms of medical organization. Large-scale healthcare, as opposed to conventional forms, was thought to have better access to financial markets and greater ability to establish capital-intensive production methods. It was considered more likely to employ professional managers to achieve those ends. The cottage industry of independent physicians was viewed as increasingly anachronistic. Still, there were many questions about how to bring more modern forms of organization to healthcare.

The committee began with only five members but grew over tenfold in the ensuing years. Physicians and institutional economists dominated membership and were influential among staff as well. The first five members consisted of Michael Davis, Lewellys Barker, formerly with Johns Hopkins School of

Medicine, Charles Winslow, a bacteriologist and founder of the Yale School of Public Health, Walton Hamilton, a leading institutional economist at the Yale School of Law, and Winford Smith, a physician and superintendent of the Johns Hopkins University hospital. Later, Lyman Wilbur served as Chair. Wilbur, a former president of the American Medical Association, was also the president of Stanford University and served as Secretary of the Interior under Hoover. Wesley Clair Mitchell, another leading institutional economist and founder of the National Bureau of Economic Research, was brought into the mix.

Institutional economists believe in a broad approach to economics that embraces a number of dimensions, including an anthropological perspective. Thorstein Veblen and Walton Hamilton are considered founders of this school of thought, which flourished in the early and mid-20th century, including at Columbia University, the University of Wisconsin at Madison, and the University of Texas at Austin. One concern many committee members shared was cultural lag. They believed the health sector culturally lagged other sectors in embracing modern large-scale efficient production, and much of the reason for it lay in the professional control of healthcare by physicians. As a result, committee deliberations were characterized by a constant tension between the need to modernize and the interests of physicians.

The committee also recognized that the health sector had a special dispensation and was infused with the mission of social and public good. In this, a purely market- and profit-driven approach was deemed inappropriate. And so, a compromise was found, that of the not-for-profit organization. The committee believed the not-for-profit form of organization would provide the latitude necessary to address the important objectives and interests of diverse stakeholders beyond efficiency, in particular access and quality. The interests of physicians were protected by recommending independent physician groups working in, but not for hospitals. This helped secure both autonomy and income. But a large group of physicians, nevertheless, dissented believing that these safeguards did not go far enough. Today, the work of the CCMC is underrecognized, but it left an indelible mark on American healthcare and set the stage for development to the current day.

The Great Depression to Post-War Period

The Great Depression was a watershed in the evolution of American healthcare. Here, the compelling issue was simple: One out of four Americans was out of work, and many others worried about job loss. Americans had to tighten their belts and many bills went unpaid. The problem was particularly pronounced in the health sector. Hospitals had a long tradition of charity care, and many Americans when deciding which bills to put off opted for hospitals and physicians. Not surprisingly, delinquent payments were much higher among hospitals compared to residential rental or mortgage payments. Charitable giving fell off as well. Something had to be done.

Calls for nationwide health insurance were nothing new in the United States. Progressives watched as national health insurance spread in Europe and they proposed that the United States follow in their footsteps. In this, they fell short, apart from bringing about workers' compensation insurance. Hospitals and physicians were wary of health insurance, fearing it would threaten their autonomy and prosperity. These were the themes that dogged the CCMC. But by the mid-1930s, things had changed. By then, hospitals and physicians were in dire straits. Now, they were more willing to embrace health insurance, but on their terms. The insurers were to be a passive payer of healthcare costs, with no rate negotiations and no interfering in the provision of care. The American Hospital Association took the lead with the establishment of Blue Cross designed to finance hospital care. Blue Shield, affiliated with the American Medical Association, soon after established similar programs to reimburse fee-for-service physician care. Blue Cross and Blue Shield plans rapidly expanded on a state-by-state basis. They were not-for-profit organizations and this protected them from state insurance premium taxes imposed on commercial insurers. It also provided some latitude to the mission to meet the interests of a wide range of stakeholders. Commercial health insurance evolved as well in this period, often focusing on insuring groups of healthy employees. This "cream skimming" facilitated large profits for the insurers and eventually undercut Blue Cross and Blue Shield that employed community rating, a single rate for all.

Prepaid healthcare where insurers assumed risk rather than passively passing on costs to employers and beneficiaries predates the Blues. Many of these organizations integrated the finance and delivery of care, but they were not embraced by the medical establishment. Indeed, there was hostility and much of the medical establishment worked to undermine prepaid plans. Health Maintenance Organizations (HMOs), as we now call them, were perceived as an affront to physician autonomy and an economic threat. An important precedent was set by the Supreme Court in 1943 when it ruled in favor of the Group Health Association (GHA) in Washington DC against the American Medical Association, finding that the Sherman Antitrust Act's provisions regarding restraint of trade had been violated. This had national implications and facilitated the growth of HMOs. The HMO Act of 1973, which among other things required larger employers to offer HMOs to employees as an option, if possible, was another major catalyst in that growth.

Tax treatment of health insurance is a very important element of the health sector today and is regarded as pivotal by economists of all stripes in explaining high levels of health spending in the United States. Its origins are in the mid-20th century. When health insurance first became widely available to employees, it was unclear whether employer contributions to health insurance constituted taxable compensation; by the 1950s, the consensus was clear that it was not. This status favored health insurance relative to other forms of compensation, especially so for those individuals with high incomes. It fueled the spread of health insurance to many more people and for many more services. This, in turn, encouraged nonprice competition as consumers paid relatively little and in the long run helped underpin the medical arms race.

The empowerment of unions during the Roosevelt and Truman administrations strengthened the bargaining position of labor. This led to the widespread inclusion of health insurance as a worker benefit, at least for those with relatively well-paid jobs. Shortages of labor during World War II accompanied by wage controls led to the use of health insurance as a recruitment and retention tool. All of this led to the rapid dissemination of private health insurance that persisted from the late 1930s until the 1970s, though it shifted toward commercial providers and away from Blue Cross and Blue Shield.

Healthcare grew even faster than the rapidly growing post-war economy. By 1960, national health expenditure as a share of GDP was 5%, up from the 3% or 4% estimated by the CCMC prior to the Great Depression. This became something of an economic issue and more economists began to turn their attention in this direction. One notable contribution in the late 1950s came from Reuben Kessel, an economist with the University of Chicago. Kessel was interested in price discrimination in the market for physician services; he observed that physician services were characterized by different prices to different patients. Those who were well-off, or with generous insurance, were charged more, while those with lesser means faced lower prices or even free care. The medical profession held up this difference as benevolent behavior and in the public interest. Kessel argued otherwise, stating that this was nothing more than veiled profit maximization. It is quite easy to show that those with monopoly power raise prices on those who are willing and able to pay more. A perfect price discriminator charges the maximum that each consumer is willing to pay, extracting all the value of exchange for themselves. Echoes of this exist today in "value-based" reimbursement schemes in healthcare, which pay providers or manufacturers the value of the goods or services on offer. Economists retort that efficient and equitable pricing is simply a price to all consumers that accords with the lowest cost of production. Value to the patient should accrue as consumer surplus, a measure of consumer welfare. Then as now, those on the supply side in healthcare prefer to extract much more of that social welfare for themselves.

Kessel's tone was perhaps a bit shrill, but other more restrained voices soon entered the fray. Milton Friedman, also at the University of Chicago in this period, questioned the role of licensure in medicine and elsewhere. He saw that licensure restricted supply and drove up prices. He accepted that those who could afford to pay received higher quality care. But what about those who could not? What is the quality of their care? Moreover, he argued that many of the restrictions had little to do with quality and were simply a means to constrain supply for the benefit of providers. Around the same time, in the early 1960s, Kenneth Arrow of Stanford wrote an article considered foundational in health economics. Arrow emphasized information asymmetries and the institutions that evolved consequently. Arrow argued that not-for-profit healthcare, affiliations with religious or philanthropic organizations, and the high degree of deference to providers help maintain faith in the legitimacy of the system. It also underpinned confidence that providers act as agents of consumers and that pecuniary excess is in check.

Medicare and Medicaid

The Progressive Movement of the late 19th and early 20th centuries advocated for national health insurance, but without much success. Franklin Roosevelt wanted it and Harry Truman made a serious but failed effort to bring it to fruition. In the post-war period, there continued to be a great deal of concern about access to healthcare for those without private health insurance. Some backstop programs were established, but the rapid expansion of private health insurance obviated the need for a national program. By the time Lyndon Johnson assumed the presidency, the political logic of pursuing Roosevelt's and Truman's objective of national health insurance seemed antiquated. But Johnson recognized a need to insure those still vulnerable, which included the elderly, the poor and unemployed, and dependents of military personnel. To that end, Johnson helped push through legislation establishing Medicare, Medicaid, and the Civilian Health and Medical Program of the Uniformed Services (CHAMPUS), programs that were a major leap in the role of the state. The advent of Medicare and Medicare in 1965 further fueled the tax-favored health sector. Private health insurance also evolved to cover not just hospital and physician services, but also retail prescription drugs. Medicare eventually followed suit, with prescription drugs, in 2006. Growth of the share of Americans with health insurance from 1940 to 1970 is shown in Figure 3.2. Health insurance was not universal but widespread by the latter 20th century.

Medicaid, which was meant to be a backstop, often temporary, for the poorest among us, has evolved to become an entitlement for the poor and lower middle class. Most of its beneficiaries are low-income adults and children but most of the expenditures are directed at the disabled and elderly. Medicaid, not Medicare, is a primary source of nursing home funding, though Medicare does provide some support upon hospital discharge.

Another important element in the latter 20th century was the Employee Retirement Income Security Act of 1974 (ERISA). ERISA provides an avenue for employers with sufficiently large pools of workers to self-insure to lower administrative costs, avoid insurance premium taxes, and avoid state insurance mandates. Self-insured employers typically hire benefit managers as

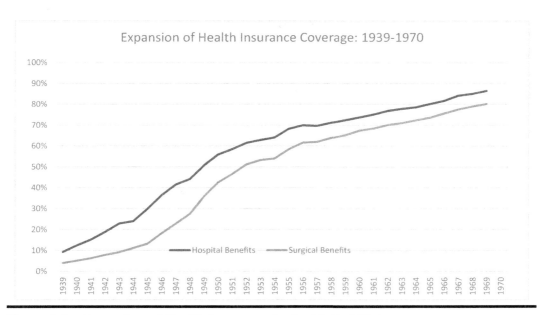

Figure 3.2   Expansion of Health Insurance in the United States

Source: US Bureau of the Census *Historical Statistics of the United States, Colonial Times to 1970* Vital Statistics and Health and Medical Care, Persons Covered by Private Health Insurance for Hospital and Surgical Benefits: 1939 to 1970, p. 82. 1975. www.census.gov/library/publications/1975/compendia/hist_stats_colonial-1970.html

third-party administrators. ERISA and the growth of federal programs such as Medicare and Medicaid has limited state health insurance regulation to a relatively small portion of the health insurance market.

The 21st Century

Health expenditures continued to rise and increase as a share of GDP in the 21st century. Figure 3.3 shows the trend from 1960 to 2020. The health sector has grown from about 5% of GDP in 1960, expanding in the wake of Medicare and Medicaid to 20% in 2020. Health spending per person in 2023 has been projected to be about $14,000. The outlook is for further increases. Economists question the efficiency of this level of spending: How can we be sure that production costs are minimized when competition is insufficient, and perhaps more importantly, that the cost of goods and services are justified by commensurate value when so much of healthcare is paid by insurers and distorted by tax incentives?

One approach to reform that has gained traction limits insurance to only the most expensive health expenditures so that consumers are incentivized to shop and weigh costs and benefits. This approach is generally

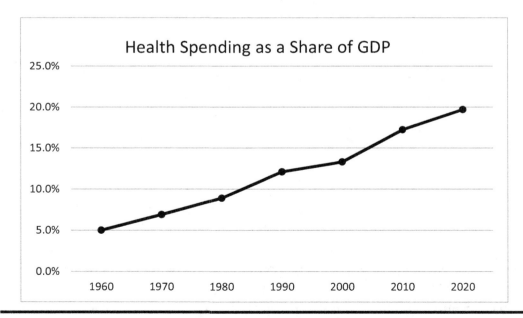

Figure 3.3   Growth of National Health Expenditures as Share of Gross Domestic Product

Sources: www.cms.gov/Research-Statistics-Data-and-Systems/Statistics-Trends-and-Reports/NationalHealthExpendData/NationalHealthAccountsProjected www.bea.gov/data/gdp

acknowledged as a helpful strategy to improve efficiency and can be achieved with high deductible plans. It was advanced in the Medicare Modernization Act of 2003, and today a large portion of the American public have high deductible plans. Sometimes, these are called consumer-driven plans that may employ tax-advantaged saving accounts purposed for out-of-pocket health expenditures along with high deductibles. The growth of such plans for single coverage with at least a $2,000 deductible is shown in Figure 3.4. Use of high deductibles is more common for employees of smaller firms but has been on the rise among firms of all sizes. A major ensuing problem that has dogged the success of consumer-driven healthcare has been price transparency. How can consumers shop when the prices they face are largely unavailable? Providers have difficulty ensuring price transparency in part because they lack adequate cost accounting systems. They have accounting systems designed for reimbursement, not management of costs. Another issue is that tax-advantaged savings plans and consumer-driven care are of much more value to higher-income Americans.

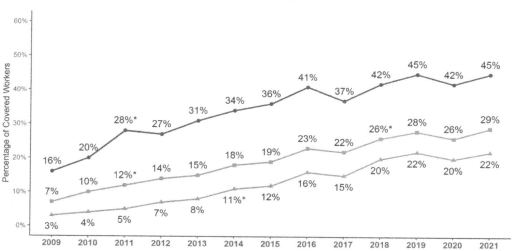

Percentage of Covered Workers Enrolled in a Plan with a General Annual Deductible of $2,000 or More for Single Coverage, by Firm Size, 2009-2021

⬤ All Small Firms   ▲ All Large Firms   ◼ All Firms

* Estimate is statistically different from estimate for the previous year shown (p < .05).

NOTE: Small Firms have 3-199 workers and Large Firms have 200 or more workers. These estimates include workers enrolled in HDHP/SOs and other plan types. Average general annual deductibles are for in-network providers.

SOURCE: KFF Employer Health Benefits Survey, 2018-2021; Kaiser/HRET Survey of Employer-Sponsored Health Benefits, 2009-2017

Figure 3.4   Growth of Consumer-Driven Health Plans

Source: 2019 Employer Health Benefits Survey, Kaiser Family Foundation, September 25, 2019 www.kff.org/report-section/ehbs-2019-section-7-employee-cost-sharing/ accessed August 18, 2021

Reprinted with permission of the Kaiser Family Foundation.

The Affordable Care Act

The United States began the 21st century with a large and technologically sophisticated health sector. It has proved to be both a primary engine of job growth and a source of dissatisfaction. The dissatisfaction can be pinned on two primary problems, excessive costs and access. American healthcare is the costliest on the planet, a widely recognized fact. And for all its expenditures, the United States has relatively poor life expectancy and infant mortality. There are several reasons for this condition, which include health behaviors. Some of these, such as high homicide and suicide rates, obesity, and drug abuse, are arguably social issues and outside the purview of the health system. Another partial explanation for relatively poor health outcomes is the lack of health insurance by millions of Americans despite the rapid spread of private and public health insurance in the 20th century. It was estimated that close to 50 million Americans were uninsured prior to the implementation of the Affordable Care Act (ACA). Most of these were low-wage earners, but not sufficiently low to qualify for Medicaid.

The problem of the uninsured has long been a subject of great political import, particularly among Democrats. The national election of 1992 had considerable focus on the twin issues of access and cost in healthcare. Following Bill Clinton's win, his administration embarked on a major effort of reform spearheaded by Hillary Clinton. Although the initiative failed, it provided important groundwork later utilized by Barack Obama. The ACA of 2010, narrowly passed on a party-line vote, led to another major expansion of federal health spending. While touted as legislation to address costs and access, most of the impact has been on the latter. A major expansion of Medicaid was a central plank of the ACA. Its intent was to cover all Americans up to 138% of the poverty level: To illustrate, a family of four with an annual income of $36,156 met the 138% threshold in 2021. States do not have to participate, but most have been drawn to covering greater numbers and accepting the federal funds associated with Medicaid expansion.

Another central element of the ACA, also known as Obamacare, is a system of health insurance exchanges designed to support the middle class. Health insurance exchanges operate in a variety of forms, but they have provided subsidies on a sliding scale up to 400% of the poverty level. So, a family of four is eligible for some assistance up to an annual income of $106,000 in 2022. Eligibility has been further eased so that individuals and families with health expenditures exceeding 8.5% of income become eligible. It is worth noting that health exchange enrollments have been hampered by adverse selection, which is to say those with the worst health are most likely to enroll. This drives up costs and premiums such that relatively healthy beneficiaries disenroll and perhaps migrate to other plans. This leaves the least healthy and most subsidized in the insurance pools. Individual mandates were meant to alleviate this problem, but they were addressed with minor penalties for noncompliance, and were in any event, eliminated as a federal requirement by 2019.

The ACA had other measures meant to expand insurance coverage such as requiring insurance plans to permit children to remain on their parents' plans until age 26, measures directed at large businesses to provide health insurance, expansion of community health centers for low-income Americans, and bans on denial of coverage for preexisting conditions. The legislation also eliminated annual and lifetime limits widely thought to be problematic by economists. The point of insurance is protection from financial ruin that annual and lifetime limits undermine. Ultimately, the ACA is recognized to have helped reduce the number of uninsured and underinsured by at least 20 million, dropping the uninsured rate among the non-elderly from 18% in 2010 to 10% in 2016.

The ACA has been less successful when it comes to cost control. An underlying premise was that lack of coordination of care is a primary driver of high cost. This idea was put forward in an article in *Health Affairs* in 2008 by Don Berwick who later served as Obama's Administrator of Medicare and Medicaid Services. Berwick saw the health sector as plagued by a lack of coordination. To counteract it, a variety of initiatives were undertaken to improve the efficiency of healthcare production. New forms of organization to better integrate hospitals, physicians, and other providers were envisioned. Accountable care organizations and medical homes are two such new forms of organization that have banked on improved coordination and costs where previous HMOs failed. Other efforts such as "value"-based and bundled payment initiatives have been undertaken along with programs to better manage dual-eligible beneficiaries in Medicare and Medicaid. More health service research has helped, and Obamacare further encouraged the drive for the use of electronic health records. All these measures have been generally applauded, but thus far cost containment outcomes have been underwhelming.

A secondary and important problem has been compounded in the wake of these efforts. Market or monopoly power in healthcare problematic before the ACA, is worse as both providers and insurers have consolidated. The reason American healthcare is so expensive, as the late Princeton Economist Uwe Reinhardt argued, is quite simply, high prices. These high prices are partially attributable to inefficient production but also to market power. The ACA only aggravated this latter worrisome problem.

One measure directed at costs and favored by economists was the Cadillac tax. It addressed the tax-favored treatment of the health sector, which was thought to be pernicious, as it led to over-insurance and excessive health spending. Outright and immediate elimination of current tax treatment would prove to be very disruptive; therefore, a "Cadillac" tax was proposed to limit tax-favored health insurance beyond a threshold associated with high-end policies. Annual policies priced above that would face a marginal tax of 40%. This quite substantial tax would encourage lower cost premiums via more efficient care and/or higher deductibles. The Cadillac tax was designed to apply to ever-increasing proportions of the American public over time with increasing pressure on the efficiency of healthcare spending. This plan was embraced by economists but loathed by insurers, providers, industry, the well-off, unions, and just about everyone who is not an economist. So, it was first designed to take effect years after implementation of the ACA, then postponed, and finally eliminated. Many of the measures designed to raise revenue and finance Obamacare were also eliminated. The access benefits of the ACA largely came to fruition, but much of the taxation for finance was not sustained, with long-run implications for the federal budget.

COVID-19

Pandemic threats from novel viruses have been anticipated since at least the time of the Spanish flu. There have been continuous viral outbreaks including more serious strains of the flu in 1957 and 1968. Viral threats were punctuated by SARS in 2002 and Ebola from 2013 to 2016. And, of course, there is the long-lasting deadly AIDS epidemic, beginning in 1981, that continues into the present day. But COVID-19 descended on the United States rapidly in 2020 and with widespread and immediate devastation. It has a mortality rate several times that of the worst outbreaks of the flu and quickly crippled the US and world economies. Mortality, but not the mortality rate, in the United States exceeds that of the Spanish flu.

History will judge our response to COVID-19 relative to that of 1918. In both cases, the primary strategy at the outset was social distancing and masks. Stay-at-home strategies were facilitated by telephones in 1918 and in the COVID era, the internet. The COVID era experienced a remarkable internet-facilitated transition to online work unimaginable in 1918. But the

virus spread nonetheless and, as in the previous era, spiked in fall and win-
ter. Unlike the Spanish flu, which devastated young adults, COVID-19 mortality was concentrated among the elderly.

Thought to have originated in an exotic animal meat market or possibly
a virology laboratory in Wuhan, China in late 2019, the virus spread to the
United States and by March 2020, widespread measures were implemented
to contain further spread. Efforts were hampered by mixed messages ema-
nating from Washington and other health authorities, poorly executed
testing, and spotty compliance with stay-at-home and other preventive recommendations. Vaccines were developed within a year, but poorly planned
and executed distribution by state and local authorities slowed the effort at
first; later, it gained momentum. Such problems underscored weakness in
public health governance. The American public, at first sidelined and scared
while federal, state, and local officials pointed fingers at each other, should
now insist on follow-up such as a blue-ribbon panel to study what went
wrong and ensure that it does not happen again in the next pandemic. For
starters, we should identify where the comparative advantage lies between
federal, state, and local government for a wide range of important functions.
These functions include prevention messaging, testing, vaccine development,
distribution, and prioritization in allocation. The study should identify lapses
in statutory authority and make recommendations to ensure that adequate
funding and resources are available to those best equipped to handle the
tasks. The best locus of decision-making and authority is not necessarily at
the federal level and there are reasons to believe local decision-making and
execution are sometimes best, particularly when local conditions are time
critical. They should be identified, adequately resourced, and include a measure of accountability.

Threats to health should also be better integrated with national defense
planning. A greater role for pandemic and other health threats should be
given greater prominence and adequately resourced in the preparations of the
Department of Defense, Central Intelligence Agency, and other organizations.
This implies some fusion of defense and health sector expertise and culture.

Another problem the COVID pandemic underscored is in the realm of
ethics and economics. Most public officials have taken the view that the
pandemic has been a health crisis and should be left to health scientists to determine what is best. This is misguided; the crisis has been largely economic,
as health and the health sector are important elements of economic welfare.
Policy measures to improve both lives and livelihoods should be sought as
win-win solutions. Unfortunately, the options are not always clear cut and

tradeoffs are sometimes required. Medical and public health authorities generally lack the training and qualifications to make such decisions. Moreover, there is an important ethical divide. Those trained in economics and business understand that costs and benefits must be weighed; those from the health sciences are loath to rely on cost as a criterion in health decisions. They regard it as unethical. But it is not. Resources are finite and there are opportunity costs to prioritization of health. Many countries recognize this and are more willing than the United States to explicitly draw the line on how much is too much in the name of health. Even the World Health Organization accepts the need for such analysis as input to resource allocation in health. The United States is exceptional in being squeamish on this account. Future pandemics can ill afford such sentiment.

Epidemiology in the 21st Century

Scholars who study long-run social trends have identified the demographic transition. It has been observed that traditional societies before the advent of modern technology had high birth and death rates, but as conditions improved, death rates fell before birth rates, leading to rapid population growth. Eventually, mature economies evolve with both low birth and death rates, and stable populations. There is another parallel transition of note called the epidemiological transition. The epidemiological transition is concerned with a shift from communicable to degenerative disease as the primary cause of morbidity and mortality. In the past, infectious disease was the major source of mortality and morbidity; but improved public health, medicine, and health behavior have greatly mitigated the threat of communicable disease. Still, the epidemiological transition will continue to unfold in future decades. Barring catastrophic pandemics of infectious disease, most Americans will die of degenerative disease. Relatively few have died of infectious disease in recent years, COVID notwithstanding, and those who have, largely succumbed to the flu and pneumonia. Figure 3.5 illustrates how death rates have declined and how infectious disease has largely disappeared compared to 1900. Heart disease, cancer, and stroke are leading sources of mortality today; but there has been remarkable diagnostic and treatment progress toward heart disease and major gains with cancer in recent decades. Other leading causes of death going forward are pulmonary disease, diabetes, kidney failure, and dementia, along with accidents and suicides. Diabetes and kidney disease, often associated with widespread

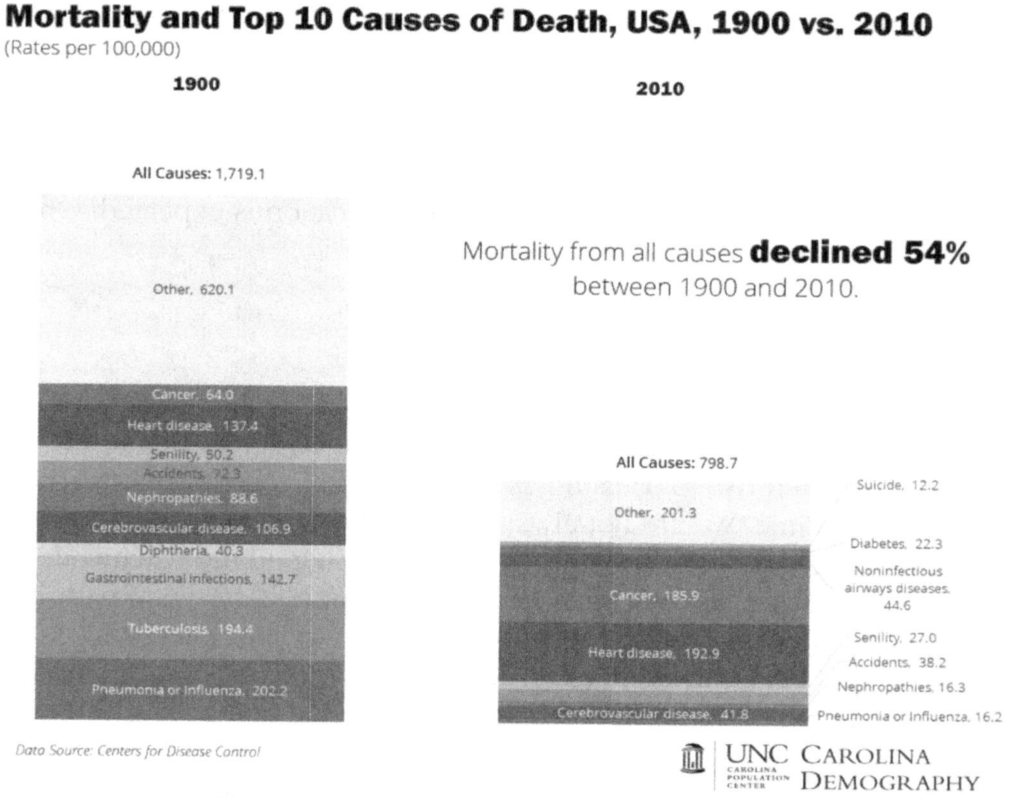

Mortality and Top 10 Causes of Death, USA, 1900 vs. 2010
(Rates per 100,000)

1900

2010

All Causes: 1,719.1

Mortality from all causes **declined 54%** between 1900 and 2010.

Other, 620.1

Cancer, 64.0

Heart disease, 137.4

Senility, 50.2
Accidents, 72.3
Nephropathies, 88.6

All Causes: 798.7

Suicide, 12.2

Cerebrovascular disease, 106.9

Other, 201.3

Diabetes, 22.3

Diphtheria, 40.3

Noninfectious airways diseases, 44.6

Gastrointestinal infections, 142.7

Cancer, 185.9

Tuberculosis, 194.4

Senility, 27.0
Accidents, 38.2

Heart disease, 192.9

Nephropathies, 16.3

Pneumonia or influenza, 202.2

Cerebrovascular disease, 41.8

Pneumonia or Influenza, 16.2

Data Source: Centers for Disease Control

UNC CAROLINA
CAROLINA POPULATION CENTER
DEMOGRAPHY

Figure 3.5   Leading Causes of Death in 1900 and 2010

Source: Figure reprinted from www.ncdemography.org/2014/06/16/mortality-and-cause-of-death-1900-v-2010/

Reprinted with permission of Carolina Demography.

obesity, remain leading public health challenges. Dementia has been on the rise recently and current treatment options are limited, making it an obvious research target going forward. COVID-19 was briefly the leading cause of death in early 2021 but then fell back behind heart disease and cancer.

Climate Change

Climate change has emerged as a top priority in the United States and around the world. It threatens livelihoods and health. Warmer temperatures have melted ice packs and brought more severe weather. Hot regions are expected to become hotter with associated health effects. More extreme droughts, wildfires, and hurricanes are anticipated with attendant health risks. Warmer temperatures, it must be noted, change the distribution of pathogens and other biological hazards. Disease-carrying insects are expected to impact regions not accustomed to these threats; cold regions, on the other hand, may welcome less-frigid conditions. Warmer temperatures will change agricultural patterns too and while some regions will benefit, others will not. The net effect is unclear, but dislocation is expected. One hopes that it will be gradual and well-managed.

Concluding Comments

The long evolution of healthcare is complex, to be sure, and rich in the institutions it has given rise to. Health has been a central concern of our species for a very long time. We are not always aware of the traditions and habits we stand upon, even as history and culture have shaped the patchwork of subsectors that make up American healthcare. The modern world with its advances in understanding and technology is of particular interest to us as it has reshaped health institutions to help provide levels of care that previous generations could scarcely imagine. The potential going forward is even greater. The next section of this book will shift gears from a historical to an economic orientation with a focus on topics that help explain why American healthcare is so exceptional and costly.

Note

1. The first Ph.D. program in Hospital and Health Administration at the University of Iowa was founded by one of Davis's students, Gerhard Hartman, after World War II. I was hired at the University of Iowa by one of Hartman's students, Samuel Levey, in the late 1980s. This was a good fit given my institutional orientation and background in health issues and the social complexity of the health sector. I had obtained an entree to health economics and management working for the Center for Naval Analyses near the Pentagon when deescalating cold war downsizing challenged Navy healthcare. It quickly became apparent that downsizing healthcare was particularly problematic since so much of military health expenditure had little to do with warfare and resulted instead from routine health services and cost pressures experienced elsewhere in the economy.

TOPICS IN HEALTH ECONOMICS

Chapter 4

Market Failure: Asymmetric Information and Monopoly Power

Asymmetric Information & Institutions

A popular theory can be a thing of beauty. The textbook world of perfect competition, for example, will lead inevitably to efficient production and allocation of resources, and for many, it is reason enough to strive for competitive markets. The world of perfect competition is characterized by an abundance of free information that consumers use to spend their money and suppliers use to decide what, how much, and when to produce. In practice, however, consumers exert considerable effort seeking information about prices and quality to better assess purchases, and suppliers must have access to technology, prices, and other information relevant to production. Significant barriers to access or to understanding relevant information may exist, and these knowledge gaps are a source of market failure. Sometimes, there is an asymmetry between the knowledge held by producers and consumers. One party may know more than the other. This is called asymmetric information and is problematic in healthcare as well as some other parts of the economy.

A well-known example of asymmetric information was described by George Akerlof of the University of California at Berkeley in a paper, published in 1970, on the used car market. Akerlof argued that sellers commonly know more about the condition of their vehicle than buyers, who are likely

DOI: 10.4324/9781003186137-6

to be suspicious when cars are marketed as being in top shape. Buyers tend to underprice offers even when cars really are in excellent condition. This dissuades sellers of high-quality cars and leads to lower average quality in the market. Used car markets have evolved since 1970, benefiting from internet technology, so that it is easier to find information about the history of vehicles or find someone with mechanical knowledge to serve as an agent for inspection. Information is now more available in the health sector too, but consumers remain handicapped by imperfect knowledge and can fall prey to marketing strategies designed to separate them from their money. Figure 4.1 depicts the age-old cliché of snake oil along with the Latin adage of caveat emptor or buyer beware.

University education is another market where consumers have been disadvantaged with cost pressures similar to those found in the health sector. How can students and parents determine the quality and suitability of institutions and educational programs? Reputation and rankings serve as proxies for quality but that has not spared graduates from buyer's remorse once they determine the limited marketability of their qualifications. There have been efforts, such as the Department of Education College Scorecard, to provide more information so that applicants can make better decisions. But there is growing unease with the value proposition in higher education. Families need to sharpen their reasons for investing in college education by making better use of information that is now increasingly available to them.

Information asymmetry is widespread in healthcare. Examples include the greater knowledge held by physicians, dentists, and pharmacists compared to the consumer or patient and the consequent concern that providers sometimes abuse this knowledge gap to induce demand for financial gain. It also exists in the health insurance market where beneficiaries usually know more about their own health than insurers do. Consumers can use this information to their advantage in the marketplace; sometimes, this leads to adverse selection when beneficiaries in poor health are drawn to insurance pools with attractive prices. This impacts the average cost of caring for the pool of beneficiaries, pushing up premiums, which leads some of the healthier beneficiaries to withdraw, or at least not renew. Premiums increase commensurate with costs, driving yet more relatively healthy beneficiaries away. Adverse selection can lead to a "death spiral" and an unsustainable model of health insurance. Insurers are very aware of this danger and design their policies accordingly to reduce such risk. For example, they commonly avoid issuing policies if the pool of beneficiaries does not have enough low-risk persons to offset high-risk ones. When it comes to rating risk, the more

Caveat Emptor

"Let the Buyer Beware"

Figure 4.1 Caveat Emptor

Source: Asymmetric Information and the Healthcare Consumer

https://commons.wikimedia.org/wiki/File:The_snake_oil_serum.jpg

Creative Commons CC 2.0

Author: Mister Serum

information insurers have the better they are able to do so. Hence, they seek information about age, geography, gender, occupation, and medical history for rate setting and benefit design. At present, insurers are constrained by laws restricting the use of genetic information, HIV status, and other categories.

Consumers face less asymmetric information now than when economists first began to explore this issue in the 1960s. There is an abundance of information available to consumers through the internet including open-access, peer-reviewed medical journals and books. A bit of online research can yield information about diagnostic and treatment options, success rates, and side effects. It can also identify new and experimental treatments including those recruiting research volunteers. Consumers are better positioned to shop for health services today and are less reliant on providers as agents to protect their welfare. But asymmetric information still exists, and some consumers have more trouble navigating this marketplace than others.

The level of education in the United States has increased substantially too. Fewer than 10% of Americans over the age of 25 had a bachelor's degree in 1960. This increased to about 38% in 2020. It goes without saying that a college degree can facilitate access and understanding of the medical and health literature.

Healthcare is commonly regarded as a domestic market with relatively little international trade outside of pharmaceuticals, medical supplies and equipment. This has changed, however, with the growth of medical tourism. Prices can be substantially lower abroad and some choose to purchase health services there, an especially attractive option for those with large deductibles or no insurance at all. It may also be an opportunity to combine healthcare with travel and leisure enjoyments. A key barrier to medical tourism, however, is information asymmetry. Consumers generally do not know about the quality of international providers and quite naturally may be suspicious of advertised claims. Consequently, international hospitals seeking American clients commonly obtain accreditation from the Joint Commission which has been accrediting and certifying American hospitals since the 1950s. Its certification of quality helps assure consumers and insurers that use of these services is safe; hence, increasingly, Americans are willing to go abroad for hospital and other forms of healthcare. Common destinations include Mexico, Thailand, and Costa Rica. Prices may be a quarter or a third of those incurred in the United States.

Agency

Markets characterized by asymmetric information commonly have agency issues. Agency refers to the use of an agent with greater expertise to act on behalf of consumers. For example, attorneys are agents for their clients as are realtors, and of course, physicians and other healthcare providers enjoy agency in their professions. They are trusted to act in the interests of the principals, their patients, and consumers when purchasing decisions are not passive. Principals (the patient/consumer) may defer decision-making authority to agents. Economists have questioned whether the interests of providers and patients align as expected, just as they also question the alignment of interests of attorneys and realtors with their clients. Agents can abuse their expertise to induce demand where benefits to the consumer do not justify the costs. An example is auto repair where consumers often worry about excessive services and charges. Another related problem arises when agents fall short of the effort expected by principals once having entered into an agreement. Consumers may believe their attorney or realtor is not working hard enough for them.

The agency relationship in healthcare has become more complex as the industry has consolidated. Increasingly, the agency relationship is with an organization rather than a person. Employees of the organization may have incentives that do not align well with that of patients and consumers; for example, they may be more concerned about their own incomes, status, and comfort than the physical, mental, or financial health of consumers. The welfare of their organization may be a very secondary concern as well, even if consumers begin to stop patronizing it.

Financial Incentives

The combination of asymmetric information, fee-for-service reimbursement, tax-protected third-party insurance, and deference to providers has provided fertile ground for the medical arms race and rapid growth of health expenditures. For some time, this has been recognized, and there have been calls to address the problem by altering financial incentives, for example, in the shift from fee-for-service to capitation where insurers and/or providers are paid a fixed rate. With capitation, there is no financial gain to induce demand; rather, the incentive is to reduce costs to increase margins. In this case, the concern is underutilization as providers seek to cut costs. Prepaid healthcare, with fixed annual or monthly payment, has a long history in the United States but was marginalized until at least the Supreme Court Decision of 1943 and probably the HMO Act of 1973. President Nixon, concerned about the rise of healthcare costs after the implementation of Medicare, was drawn to a form of prepaid healthcare called health maintenance organizations (HMOs) by Paul Ellwood of the University of Minnesota and Interstudy, a think tank. Ellwood argued that HMOs, characterized by the integration of finance and delivery, would improve efficiency. Nixon was persuaded by this promise and sought to promote HMOs by supporting the HMO Act. This included a movement toward Medicare HMOs, now called Medicare Advantage plans, which had a market share of 42% of enrollees in 2021. One of the central ways in which HMOs contain costs is with selective contracting among a narrow network. Providers are assured volume in exchange for favorable rates. A related managed care form, the preferred provider organization (PPO), does not typically use capitation and instead relies primarily on selective contracting with reduced network fee-for-service rates.

Capitation has had problems over time including an unwillingness of providers to accept them. In the 1990s, many hospitals and physicians were hurt by accepting risks associated with capitation. Costs tend to rise as capitated programs expand: Although the first to join such schemes tend to be the relatively healthy who do not use many health services, the latecomers are less healthy. The case of Medicare is instructive. The first to join Medicare HMOs were the relatively healthy elderly. Over time, as more participated in HMOs, average costs rose, and this caused Medicare Choice, President Clinton's variant of Medicare HMOs, to derail in the late 1990s. Insurers withdrew from the market as reimbursement rates were unattractive relative to higher costs. The program known as Medicare Part C was reorganized as Medicare Advantage and it had more attractive reimbursement following the Medicare Reorganization Act of 2003 enacted under President George W. Bush. Medicare reimbursement also evolved to better adjust for risk, and this helped attract insurers to the Medicare Advantage market.

Another problem has been competition based on managed risk, not managed care. HMOs and insurers more generally have put much effort into screening for healthy beneficiaries, or at least those less likely to use healthcare, rather than managing health services efficiently. In fact, insurers are much more comfortable managing risk than healthcare.

In recent years, many physicians have shifted away from both fee-for-service and capitation toward salaries. This change corresponds to consolidation in the industry and the advantage of larger organizations providing health information technology and bargaining power with insurers. It also corresponds with social changes with more female physicians and a greater desire for better work-life balance. In salaried settings, there is less incentive for induced demand and less incentive to cut corners; but as with all salaried workers, there may be a tendency to limit labor absent monitoring and performance measurement.

Agency relationships require trust, and health sector institutions have evolved accordingly. The not-for-profit healthcare organization, commonly with religious affiliation, has been a mainstay in the American health sector particularly among hospitals, hospital groups, and long-term care organizations. Single-minded pecuniary gain ahead of patient well-being is not the expectation most consumers have of such organizations. The equity of not-for-profits is held by the "community" and trustees have some latitude to allow a management focus on stakeholders rather than shareholders. Stakeholders include patients but also the workforce and local community. Not-for-profit organizations are required to provide charity care and community service to maintain their favored status with the Internal Revenue Service (IRS). The IRS requires detailed information specifying what charity is being provided; although much of the "charity" is acceptance of public sector reimbursement rates. The not-for-profit status also facilitates tax-advantaged donations to endowments and trusts as well as access to municipal bond markets for raising capital. Many economists have been skeptical of the utility of widespread not-for-profit status in healthcare, arguing that social welfare would be enhanced with greater tax revenue and more efficient production associated with for-profit governance. But relatively few nondistressed healthcare organizations convert from not-for-profit to for-profit status because management is better off without elevated return on equity pressure and taxes. For-profit hospitals have better access to capital markets and are more common in the south as shown in Figure 4.2. Cultural and regulatory factors may help explain this.

Monopoly and Market Power

Monopoly power refers to pricing and other discretion that sole suppliers have in the marketplace. A broader definition includes the ability suppliers with market power have, even if they are not the sole supplier, to raise prices without loss of most, or all, sales. It can extend to the buyers' market too which is sometimes called monopsony power. A sole buyer has power over the price paid and this power also exists in concentrated markets with more than one buyer.

Economic theory holds that monopoly power generally leads to reduced output and higher prices. It also results in a shift of welfare from consumers to producers as consumers pay more and suppliers enjoy greater profit.

Hospitals by Ownership Type: For-Profit, 2019

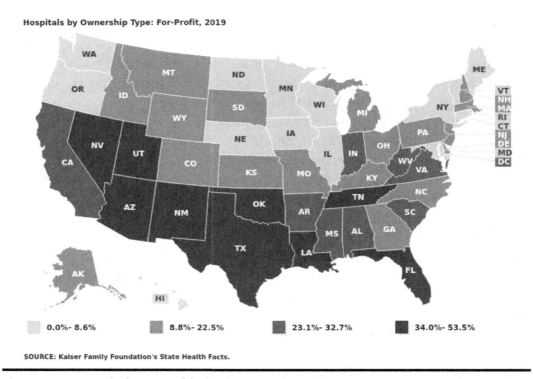

0.0%- 8.6%	8.8%- 22.5%	23.1%- 32.7%	34.0%- 53.5%

SOURCE: Kaiser Family Foundation's State Health Facts.

Figure 4.2   Hospital Ownership in the United States

Source: https://www.kff.org/other/state-indicator/hospitals-by-ownership/?current Timeframe=1&sortModel=%7B%22colId%22:%22Location%22,%22sort%22:%22asc%22%7D Accessed August 18, 2021.

Reprinted with permission of the Kaiser Family Foundation.

Market power may facilitate price discrimination with higher prices for those with greater and more inelastic demand and lower prices for those more sensitive to price. This generates an even greater shift of consumer welfare to producers. Price discrimination is commonplace, such as discounts for students or retirees. Monopsony power occurs where the number of buyers is limited. Monopsony power is expected to result in sustained underpayment to sellers relative to competitive markets.

The issue of sustained profits in monopolies has long been a topic of debate by economists. There is a common economic assumption of profit maximization as the primary or sole objective of the business organization. This has been called into question, particularly for larger organizations where ownership and control are separated. Managers of large organizations serve as agents for owners who commonly seek profit. But managers have other interests such as their own salaries, prestige, and lifestyle, and they may not pursue profits to the exclusion of other objectives. Sir John Hicks, a Nobel Prize–winning economist, once quipped that the "best of all monopoly profits is a quiet life." In practice, this usually means that advantages conferred by monopoly power may result in a higher cost structure rather than profits. Organizations may use the slack that monopoly power affords to overstaff, overpay, and otherwise overresource their operations. This results in high costs rather than maximized sustained high profits.

There is another variant of monopoly theory with great relevance to the health sector. It is called monopolistic competition and was first put forward in 1933 by Edward Chamberlain in *The Theory of Monopolistic Competition*. Chamberlain drops the assumption of commodity-like markets assumed in perfect competition and monopoly and argues that many, if not most, markets have heterogeneous output. Markets for agricultural products such as wheat or corn resemble these homogeneous outputs. The output of one producer is much the same as another. But many markets are characterized by much more heterogeneous output with a wide range of variants available. These markets are not commodity-like; rather, consumers are faced with variations in quality and other characteristics. Asymmetric information is often present with consumers unable to fully distinguish quality, and producers use this to their advantage to differentiate products or services to appeal to perceived quality and taste. Such markets lend themselves to the use of new technology to signal better quality as well as marketing and advertising to influence perceptions. Entry into such markets by new firms is possible, unlike in monopoly, and may be quite easy. The threat of entry disciplines the markets as suppliers restrain prices to discourage competition. Common examples of such markets include automobiles, breakfast cereals, laundry detergents, restaurants, and clothing where there are multiple differentiated consumer choices.

Monopolistic competition is characterized by several or even multiple firms with differentiated products. Each has some monopoly power over their brand or variant. Use of patents, trademarks, and branding is common, and unlike commodity markets, suppliers can raise prices without losing all sales. These markets tend toward nonprice competition to improve perceived product or service quality. This in turn drives up costs, especially in the long run. They exhibit innovation ranging from wasteful differentiation to important breakthrough technologies with great social value.

The healthcare sector is very much characterized by monopolistic competition. Relatively few subsectors are commodity-like. Eyeglasses and contact lenses along with generic drugs, with commonly perceived quality parity among competing brands, and generic over-the-counter medication are commodities to a great extent. But hospital and physician services, dental care, and branded pharmaceuticals are all examples of markets where consumers must select based on perceived quality differences. They often do so with tax-advantaged health insurance paying much of the cost, which renders price sensitivity relatively ineffective. So, they opt for perceived quality without much regard for cost. Over the long run, this has fueled a medical arms race driving up the cost structure of healthcare products and services and along with it, prices. On the more positive side, the rising cost structure contributed to the development and diffusion of very important lifesaving and life-improving technologies that have benefited not just the United States but the entire world.

Monopolistic competition does not work so well when a consolidated national health insurer prevails. National health insurers are less willing to indulge new technologies without substantial added value and they use their monopsony power to drive down reimbursement to providers. This may help explain why the United States with a high level of fragmented private health insurance (around half of health expenditures) spends so much compared to other nations. Figure 4.3 plots per capita income adjusted for purchasing power currency rates against health expenditures as a share of GDP.

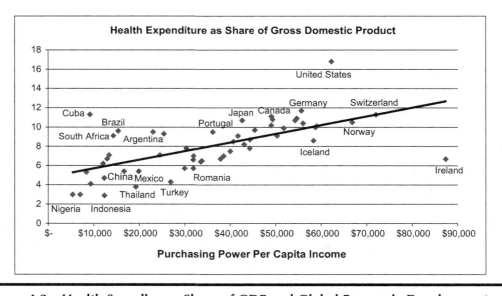

Figure 4.3 · Health Spending as Share of GDP and Global Economic Development

Source: World Bank, World Development Indicators, accessed various dates

As can be seen, there is a clear trend upward with high levels of prosperity corresponding to a greater allocation of the economy to health. There is also much variation around that trend, with the United States a very clear outlier.

There are other explanations for relatively high or low levels of health spending. Cuba has put a high priority on health spending, for example. Results can be driven more by the denominator. Some countries, such as Ireland, have high levels of GDP because of tax advantages that draw industry, and Norway's GDP is influenced greatly by fossil fuel wealth. Economic growth rates can be important. Rapidly growing countries such as Indonesia and Turkey have not allocated sufficient resources to the health sector to keep up with the brisk growth in GDP. There are multiple explanations for why countries place where they do.

High levels of American health spending raise the question of health outcomes: Perhaps, the spending levels can be justified by better results. However, this is difficult to establish. The United States does have some favorable outcomes for cancer and other medical procedures relative to other developed countries and it is an engine of new technology, but population-based measures like life expectancy and infant mortality do not compare well. More will be said of this in Chapter 8.

Price Competition

Americans generally do not use more health services than residents of other countries. Prices are the primary reason the United States is such an outlier in Exhibit 3. In many parts of the American health sector, price competition is not working well. Prices in the health sector have generally increased faster than economy-wide prices or the inflation rate. Other factors drive health spending too and they include utilization rates, the intensity of care, population increase, and demographic factors such as an aging population. The Center for Medicare and Medicaid Services has projected that healthcare prices will outstrip economy-wide prices in the period from 2019 to 2028. Bear in mind, prices were already very high in 2019, so this growth is on top of a high base. Rising health prices are expected to be the single most important factor for increasing personal health expenditures followed by increased utilization and intensity of care, population growth, and the age-sex mix.

Monopoly power resulting from consolidation is part of the reason. Providers have banded together to gain more bargaining power with insurers. The advent of health information technology, particularly in the second decade of the 21st century, further fueled provider mergers and acquisitions to gain the necessary size. Recent hospital consolidation is shown in Figure 4.4. The number and particularly the size of organizations joining together have increased. There has been consolidation among private insurers too and public insurers such as Medicare and Medicaid have been rapidly growing and exerting more influence in the marketplace.

Physicians have been rapidly consolidating as well. Most physicians no longer own their own practices, opting instead to join groups better able to provide the technology and other support necessary in the changing environment. The groups they join have been growing and many are affiliated with or owned by hospital groups.

Healthcare markets tend to be regional and there can be substantial monopoly or monopsony power at that level. California, for example, is characterized by significant monopsony power held by Delta Dental, which has considerable power over prices. Dental groups are smaller and less able to advantageously negotiate rates. Private dental insurance is also less widespread and less comprehensive than medical insurance. Moreover, Medicare and Medicaid offer relatively little for dental coverage. This helps explain why dental spending has remained low and slipped as a share of national health expenditures.

Healthcare in the United States has become increasingly concentrated, a worrisome trend. In theory, a bilateral monopoly where there is one

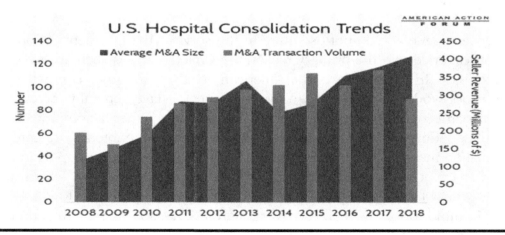

Figure 4.4 Consolidation in the American Hospital Industry

Source: www.americanactionforum.org/weekly-checkup/the-state-of-state-medicaid-expansion/

Author: Ryan Haygood

Reprinted with permission of American Action Forum.

provider, and one insurer can yield favorable results consistent with a competitive market as each party wields countervailing power over the other. This logic can extend to countervailing power in more oligopolistic structures with multiple organizations having market power. In practice, this is unlikely, and consumers can expect both providers and insurers to gain at their expense.

Does Competition Work to Contain Cost in the Health Sector?

Monopolistic competition has interesting implications for competition and antitrust policy. The health sector is especially problematic because third-party insurance is so widespread. Nonprice competition, which is a primary characteristic of monopolistic competition, has led to higher prices as firms embrace expensive new technologies, high-cost providers, and extensive infrastructure. Studies have shown that increasing the number of competitors in such an environment drives up prices rather than down. This was pointed out to the medical community in a 1987 article in the *Journal of the American Medical Association* (JAMA), which found that hospital prices were on average 15% greater in markets with more competitors. Under such conditions, there is an argument for more concentrated market structures with fewer competitors. On the other hand, when price competition prevails, less market concentration leads to lower prices, as one would expect. Medicare payment reform beginning in the 1980s has lessened the impulse toward nonprice competition and studies of selective contracting where managed care divisions of insurers negotiate with providers over price in exchange for volume demonstrate considerable success in shifting toward price competition. Narrow networks with more limited choices have afforded lower costs and lower premiums to beneficiaries.

Providers have objected to selective contracting, arguing that it reduces choice by precluding many providers from participating. This, they argue, is anticompetitive. In many states, any willing provider or freedom of choice legislation has been implemented to contain selective contracting. These laws most commonly apply to HMO networks and pharmacies.

To summarize, competition works in healthcare when there are incentives to contain costs, but it may be associated with narrower choices. Accordingly, public policy should facilitate price competition. For this, the Justice Department's Antitrust Division and the Federal Trade Commission have primary authority at the federal level; they have had a keen interest in the health sector since at least the late 1980s and have concentrated much of their effort there. They have enforced price fixing in physician service markets where competitors agree to high prices. They have closely monitored hospital and physician group mergers and acquisitions and have moved to block or modify some of them. They have also intervened in health insurance markets. Their success in court has been mixed, with wins and losses. Courts recognize that greater concentration tends toward greater monopoly power and that this can lead to higher prices. But there are efficiency arguments for consolidation too, and one is the failing firm argument. What if a hospital were to fail absent acquisition by a larger rival? Probable firm failure makes anticompetitive outcomes difficult to establish. There are also efficiencies in production that may result from consolidation even if firm failure is not part of the scenario. Courts may be receptive to arguments about reduction in duplication of cancer or heart care capacity or efficiencies in health information technology. Despite the efforts of antitrust authorities, consolidation in the health sector has continued albeit with heightened requirements for financial and operational integration.

Antitrust is not limited to the federal domain. State authorities can intervene to enforce competition laws. California found that hospital prices were higher in northern California than elsewhere and concluded this was largely the result of the contracting practices of Sutter Health, a dominant hospital network. Contractual prices between insurers and hospitals can be widely divergent and are driven by the market and negotiating power of the respective parties. California eventually reached a settlement with Sutter Health; among other things, it permitted insurers to negotiate with a subset of Sutter Hospitals rather than the entire group.

Consumer-driven insurance policies with high deductibles are an important tool to shift the health sector from nonprice to price competition. The number of Americans covered by such policies has grown sharply in recent years. Health insurance exchanges associated with the ACA have high deductibles as do many health insurance options offered by employers. Research indicates that utilization of health services declines when consumers have high deductibles, though tax-advantaged health savings accounts mitigate the impact, and may increase spending for those in very high-income brackets. No doubt the availability of better information about price and quality would help improve consumer decisions and ultimately economic efficiency. Markets such as the eyecare sector, where prices are more readily available, facilitate consumer choice compared to hospital or physician services where price and quality information are more difficult to obtain.

It is hard to blame the public for skepticism regarding price competition in the health sector because it has not worked well. Competition in healthcare has generated a very innovative sector with valuable new technology but at extremely high cost. The importance of innovation and new technology should not be minimized, but there is an alternative to high costs and high levels of innovation. It is innovation with lower costs, which is all too rare in the health sector. We should not assume that price competition cannot work well in healthcare simply because it has not in the past. Institutional change has the potential to alter the trajectory of how technology evolves. Many economists question our regime of patent protection. Patents confer monopoly protection for an extended period. Perhaps, greater use of grants and prizes would generate more innovation at lower cost in pharmaceuticals, medical equipment, and elsewhere. It could also reduce wasteful differentiation with little added value. Encouragement of a greater awareness of price by consumers via the availability of more price and quality information is another broadly supported change. More competitive labor markets would be another. Widespread use of cost-effectiveness criteria to help determine how much is too much is yet another. But perhaps the greatest potential lies in new cost-saving technologies ranging from telehealth, sensors combined with mobile phone and household applications, and artificial intelligence. Such technology, if employed to improve health and reduce costs, could transform the health sector into an engine of both growth and productivity. These are some of the issues explored in subsequent chapters.

Chapter 5

Occupational Licensure and Control

Economics of Occupational Licensure

Many occupations are subject to licensure. There are two primary reasons for this, and the first has to do with information asymmetry. Consumers commonly do not know, and often have difficulty establishing, if workers in various occupations are suitably qualified. Occupational licensure, usually designed to vet workers for appropriate levels of education and experience, helps screen out the dubiously credentialed, from borderline charlatans to outright quacks, assuring the public that the agents they hire have appropriate qualifications and skills. Licensure is an institutional means to address market failure.

The second reason for occupational licensure is the effective vehicle it presents for protecting occupational incumbents from competitive pressures. Occupational organizations advocate for high quality in their services as a matter of necessity to protect public welfare. Conveniently, this goes hand-in-hand with erecting and maintaining substantial barriers to entry. Barriers might include many years of formal education, internships, testing, and other means of limiting entry to a given occupation. Occupational licensure is an effective barrier because practicing without a license is illegal, and the apparatus of the state thus serves to enforce the law and thereby constrain supply. The result is economic rents for protected occupations and higher prices for consumers. Economic rent refers to revenue earned greater than the amount necessary for efficient production and allocation of goods and services.

DOI: 10.4324/9781003186137-7

To be sure, there is merit to the first argument. The public often needs protection from purveyors of dubious claims and assurance that those they hire are appropriately qualified. Economists, however, tend to be suspicious of this reasoning and commonly believe the second argument is the stronger one. Why? In part, because the most vociferous advocates for occupational control come not from the public but rather the occupations themselves. And when those controls are examined, they seem most strongly directed at new entrants, not the occupation they hope to join. Studies bear this out. Restrictions are commonly grandfathered to not impact incumbents with little, if any, expectation of quality assurance for them. For example, once licensed, healthcare providers are only expected to complete periodic continuing education that commonly lacks rigor or impact. This often exists side by side with enthusiastic support for greater educational, testing, and practice requirements for new entrants. We also observe licensing boards generally comprised mostly of members from the occupations with perhaps token outsider representation of consumer and other interests. This leads to an "in group" mentality adversely impacting disciplinary measures against errant providers or others subject to regulatory control. Those outside the group, even those with relevant expertise, are often considered unqualified to pass judgment on occupational matters. There is much greater interest in pursuing and penalizing unlicensed than licensed low-quality providers. The problem exists in occupational self-regulation too, where codes of conduct are promulgated by professional associations and other related groups but enforcement of penalties for misconduct is rarely vigorous.

Occupational turf wars over the scope of practice are another consequence of licensure. Overlapping skills and services can lead to conflict in which the public interest is often given short shrift. Healthcare providers of various stripes often furnish the same services. For example, nurse practitioners and physicians both provide primary care, pharmacists and physicians immunize, and physicians prescribe eye medication as do optometrists in some cases. Nurse practitioners, pharmacists, and optometrists can be interchangeable in the provision of some services; indeed, quality is often higher when provided by alternative providers.

Occupational control is an important professional vehicle serving the interests of those subject to regulation. This is consistent with the capture theory of regulation which consistently shows that regulation commonly serves the interests of those regulated. This occurs largely because of the concentrated interest in regulation by those most impacted and the more diffused and less impactful interests of the public. Members of the public may be welcome at regulatory meetings, but their attendance is usually scant. On the other hand, industry and occupational representatives are much more likely to appear well-prepared to state their case. Over time, these concentrated interests tend to prevail, in part because of a general absence of interest and engagement from the public.

Some economists, such as Milton Friedman, have argued that there is an alternative to licensure that can serve free markets and address information asymmetries. Friedman asserted that licensed occupations should use certification instead. Consumers could choose between certified and noncertified professionals. Certified workers would complete the requisite education, testing, and experience that many consumers prefer. Noncertified workers may lack this background but offer lower prices for services. They may also be well-qualified for what they do, even if not certified.

Profile of Occupational Control in the United States

Occupation licensure is widespread in the United States, especially in the service sector and the upper ranks of educational preparation. It is found in healthcare, law, education, engineering, and many other sectors. Figure 5.1 shows the percentage of occupations licensed in different sectors of the American economy. At the top of the list, the highest fraction with licensure is healthcare practitioners. Healthcare support occupations, such as nursing assistants, phlebotomists, and home health aides, are fourth in terms of licensure. Figure 5.2 provides a granular view of licensure within the healthcare community. As can be seen, licensure is clearly widespread and most commonly found where higher levels of education are required.

Geographic Variation

Rent-seeking or income-boosting behavior by occupations occurs nationwide but licensure is subject to geographic variation. Some states are more inclined to regulate by licensing than others. Figure 5.3 shows the geographic distribution that appeared in a White House report in 2015. As can be seen, there is no clear pattern in the distribution, but Iowa, Nevada, and Washington had the highest share of workers licensed, and South Carolina had the lowest. Overall, more than a quarter of American workers were licensed, far more than the 12% unionized in 2020. This is up from about 5% of the workforce who were licensed in 1950. The White House report also found persuasive evidence that occupational licensure undermines

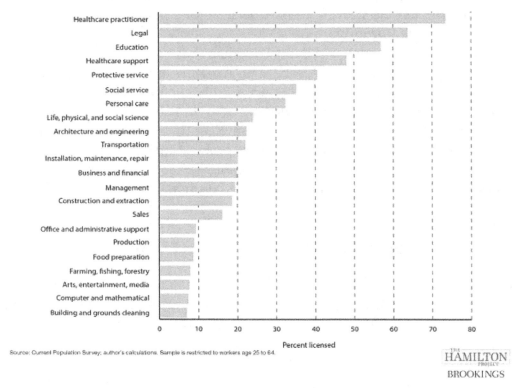

Figure 5.1   Percentage of Occupations Licensed

Source: https://www.brookings.edu/research/occupational-licensing-and-the-american-worker/

Reprinted with permission of the Brookings Institution.

employment and generates sustained higher wages at all income levels for licensed workers, averaging 10% to 15% more than unlicensed workers after adjusting for education and other relevant variables. They found occupational licensure more commonplace over time because of a shift to more licensed services and more occupations requiring licensure. Yet, the White House report found no consistent improvements in quality associated with stricter licensure. In many cases, there was none.

Impact of Occupational Control on Wages

One of the most important impacts of occupational control is elevated incomes. Barriers to entry tend to limit supply and licensure, along with

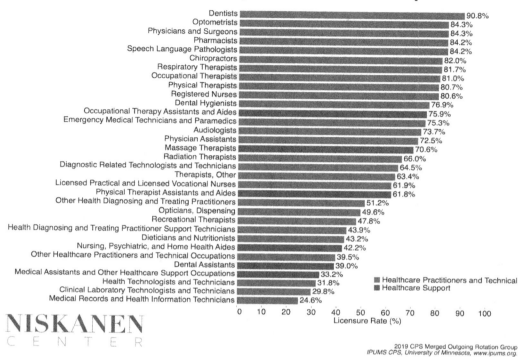

Figure 5.2 Licensure Rate within Healthcare

Source: https://www.niskanencenter.org/wp-content/uploads/2020/05/Health-care-licensing.pdf

Reprinted with permission of the Niskanen Center.

Author: Robert Orr

supply in turn puts upward pressure on prices that are ultimately borne by consumers. Licensure requirements are more common for those with advanced degrees compared to high school graduates. The boost to wages is higher too. Physicians in the United States with many years of study and training, for example, have benefited from existing institutions and earn much more than most Americans, even most of those with advanced degrees.

Most health providers are subject to licensure, and this includes physicians, dentists, pharmacists, and nurses. Generally, educational expectations in the healthcare sector are high in the United States and have been since the Flexner era, and they continue to evolve with higher educational hurdles

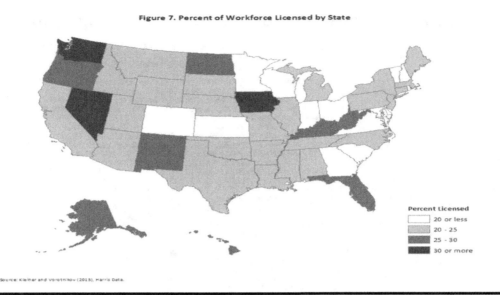

Figure 7. Percent of Workforce Licensed by State

Percent Licensed
- 20 or less
- 20 - 25
- 25 - 30
- 30 or more

Source: Kleiner and Vorotnikov (2015), Harris Data.

Figure 5.3   Geographic Distribution of Licensed Workers in the United States in 2015

Source: The While House with support from the Department of the Treasury, Council of Economic Advisors and the Department of Labor https://obamawhitehouse. archives.gov/sites/default/files/docs/licensing_report_final_nonembargo.pdf p.24

to advancement. For example, new pharmacy graduates could practice with a bachelor's degree until the 1990s; now, they must obtain a doctorate in pharmacy (PharmD) to do so. There have been similar evolutions in other occupations, such as physical therapy and audiology. There is ongoing pressure to require that all registered nurses obtain a bachelor's degree in nursing and, at the same time, to terminate associate degree programs in nursing offered by community colleges. It is not clear the extent to which more education improves quality; studies are mixed and rarely address whether any additional quality justifies added costs. But higher levels of education benefit universities by generating more revenue opportunities. Figure 5.4 shows that healthcare providers rank fourth in the boost to incomes afforded by licensure while healthcare support occupations rank first. These premiums are adjusted for education, experience, and other independent variables affecting earnings.

Certification is widespread in healthcare along with licensure. The certification of physicians, for example, requires considerable work beyond the medical degree and licensure. Licensure alone may be insufficient for career advancement. Most medical graduates become residents where they gain expertise in specialties ranging from primary care fields such as family

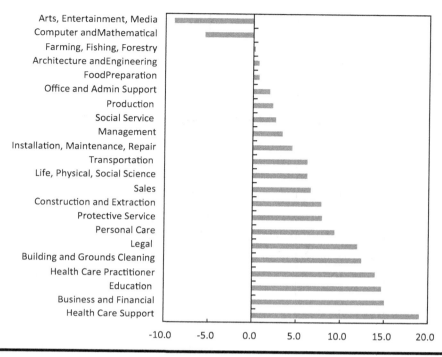

Figure 5.4   Wage Effect of Licensure by Occupation

Source: The While House with support from the Department of the Treasury, Council of Economic Advisors and the Department of Labor https://obamawhitehouse. archives.gov/sites/default/files/docs/licensing_report_final_nonembargo.pdf p64

medicine and pediatrics to more tertiary specialties such as otolaryngology (ear, nose, and throat) and ophthalmology (eyes). They then gain certification in these specialties. Many medical positions with healthcare organizations require board certification in at least one specialty. Even so, it has not been a violation of the law for a physician to practice without certification. Medical residents, for example, practice without it. Other occupations, too, may specialize with or without certification. Pharmacists are increasingly specializing in areas such as infectious disease, oncology, and gerontology. Nurses have a wide range of specialization as well. The case for occupational licensure in healthcare must rest on real and cost-justified improvements in quality relative to freer markets. Studies of occupational licensure yield questionable results. The case for licensing anesthesiologists, for example, is easily made. But what about athletic trainers, barbers, and interior designers who have licensure requirements in various states? One may be surprised to learn that manure applicators in Iowa, junkyard dealers in Ohio, and fortune-tellers in Maryland have been subject to state licensure Common sense leads one to question the necessity of public intervention to address market failure in these cases. State licensure authorities rarely subject their regulation to cost–benefit analysis.

Other Adverse Impacts of Occupational Licensure

State occupational regulation also serves as an impediment to the free movement of human resources across state lines, thus undermining the efficiency of the national economy. One state does not always have reciprocal recognition of licensure with other states, which constrains interstate migration. Fortunately, the existence of a nursing licensure compact now helps to ease interstate movement; 34 states participated in this compact in 2021, and others are pending. Physicians similarly have an interstate medical license compact, with 29 state participants in 2021 and others pending. These arrangements facilitate not only migration but also the growth of telemedicine.

Occupational licensure often imposes barriers to those with criminal records; many regulators will not license such individuals. They rarely assess the risks and benefits of those released from prisons working in the occupations they regulate. Because such restrictions undermine economic efficiency, income distribution, and social justice, advocates have made calls for a more receptive approach to those with a criminal history.

To be sure, the equity implications of occupational licensure are important. Licensure can bolster the incomes of lower-income individuals and households. But entry barriers and restrictions to theoretically maintain high levels of quality have an adverse impact on other low-income segments of the population. The "Cadillac" effect of high-quality care may work well for those with generous insurance or who can otherwise afford it, but less prosperous consumers are often priced out of participation. The quality of their care can be seriously compromised if they have no access to adequately trained providers. Limited supply imposes nonprice costs too. Constrained numbers of providers undermine staffing in less desirable locations, which may impose geographic costs on lower-income groups as they have to travel farther to receive care. Fewer providers may lead to longer wait times both to get appointments and to be seen after arrival. Studies have found such inconvenience to be a significant factor in the demand for health services. To make matters worse, with licensure barriers the occupational options of lower-income Americans may be narrowed to lower-wage generating fields;

entry restrictions for higher-paying licensed occupations divert them to lower-paying, less protected employment.

In the long run, the most important factor for economic growth and prosperity is productivity, and improved productivity depends very much on innovation. Economists generally believe that occupational licensure retards innovation. It is no surprise that the stewards of occupations are not well disposed toward labor-saving technology that undermines the demand for their services. For example, the implementation of telemedicine has been slow to move forward, and occupational resistance was only really overcome recently when COVID forced this issue. In addition, artificial intelligence will almost certainly meet a measure of resistance as will any technological or organizational innovation threatening the welfare of incumbents. This problem is more acute in sectors such as healthcare that have a large potential for economy-wide impact. In sum, it must be noted that productivity growth in the United States slowed in recent decades and that occupational licensure is part of the explanation for this deceleration.

Policy and Reform

Politically, there is growing bipartisan recognition of the adverse impact of excessive state licensure of occupations and louder calls for states to subject such regulation to cost–benefit analysis. The COVID-19 epidemic accelerated deregulation in the healthcare sector as shortages of manpower forced many states to ease restrictions on out-of-state providers, at least on a temporary basis—a shift facilitated by the federal Department of Health and Human Services. Perhaps, some of this easing will be permanent.

Residency requirements for migrant healthcare professionals are a common barrier to entry for both interstate and international movements. Many occupations require in-state residency for a defined period as a prerequisite to acquire licensure. It is hard to see how this requirement protects the public; rather, it seems a deterrent for migrants. International medical graduates (IMGs) are an important part of the physician workforce. Generally, IMGs earn a bachelor's degree in medicine in their home country and then come to the United States for their residencies. State medical societies award them an MD equivalence based on their bachelor's degree if they pass a licensure exam. It should be noted that public awareness of the differences between US and international medical education is scant. Perhaps, the public has a right to know who among the physicians—some of whom may treat them—really has been through a doctoral curriculum in medicine. IMGs account for about a quarter of the physician workforce and occupy positions well-qualified American students would like to hold. Currently, the demand for physicians is not being met by the output of MD programs within the United States, although the growth of osteopathic medical programs has helped. A small part of the total in 1970, osteopathic programs have expanded rapidly. Most are private and tuition-driven, unlike many of the MD programs which are more reliant on research funding and patient revenue, a fact that makes osteopathic programs relatively responsive to the market. Students of osteopathic medicine now account for about a quarter of those enrolled in medical programs.

Although the need for cost–benefit analysis of state occupational licensure is apparent, the issue has not caught on with the public as a compelling topic deserving their attention. Not surprisingly, it remains anathema to the occupations. It is not clear whether there will be meaningful engagement from state policy-makers to generate the needed reform. Even so, the federal government can take the lead toward reform in a limited way. The Obama administration allocated funds to support state research for improved occupational licensure. This includes the application of cost–benefit analysis, the use of certification as an alternative, and a general reduction of occupational barriers. Some of these barriers can be quite formidable. For example, the White House report found that licensure in Hawaii required 724 days, on average, to meet requirements to gain licensure, a condition that might have more to do with keeping mainlanders out than assuring quality. The Trump and Biden administrations have also been concerned about occupational licensure and followed-up by advocating for reform. A recent approach has the Federal Trade Commission reviewing state restrictions on interstate occupational mobility.

Providing assurance to the consuming public sometimes requires great subtlety, and in matters of healthcare quality, it is particularly difficult. Still, the demand for assurance can be met in a variety of ways. Licensure is one of them, but other means exist too. Certification was mentioned, but seals of approval and branding are also important ways to provide assurance. Some sectors of the economy rely on guarantees and warranties; while less common in healthcare, this approach is of increasing importance. Word of mouth can be important as are reputations of schools and institutions associated with providers as well as published rankings of quality and satisfaction. Referrals from trusted sources are yet another form of assurance. More recently, the internet has afforded greater access to quality-related information via computers and cell phones.

Final Comments on Occupational Licensure

The effect of occupational control on social welfare has long been a matter of debate. Adam Smith, in his *Wealth of Nations*, was clear about the detrimental impact of occupational guilds that evolved from the medieval period. Concerned about the associations of people from the same trade, Smith noted that "People of the same trade seldom meet together, even for merriment and diversion, but the conversation ends in a conspiracy against the public, or in some contrivance to raise prices." This statement is usually interpreted by economists as a critique of monopoly behavior, but it was primarily an observation of occupational control, albeit in the context of 18th-century western economies. Today, there is widespread recognition of the impact of unions on employment, wages, and prices, and unions have lost much of their clout in the private sector. They have been in decline for decades, notwithstanding renewed interest as a means of addressing income distribution. But occupational licensure, with a similar impact, has been on the rise and largely out of the public eye. It is rare to see bipartisan support for anything in this era of partisan bickering, but it is promising that Washington now supports reform of occupational control. Reform measures include subjecting existing and proposed licensure to cost–benefit analysis, which would include a review of the scope of practice and entry requirements ranging from education, experience, residency, and testing. Reform should also address membership of the licensure boards to shift control away from the occupations themselves. Most of this must occur at the state level; the federal government is largely constrained and limited to persuading and offering economic incentives. In some cases, Medicare and Medicaid funding could be made contingent on reform, which would surely get the attention of policy-makers in state capitals.

Economics of the Corporate Practice of Medicine

The CCMC did much to lay the foundation of modern American healthcare. The committee recognized the need for large-scale production and improved productivity via new technology, but it was fractured between economists and physicians—a nearly unbridgeable divide as it turned out. The latter were very concerned about physician autonomy and feared the corporatization of American medicine, which they believed would compromise their autonomy and economic well-being as well as the health of their patients.

Economists feared that too much physician control would drive up costs and retard innovation. The committee did reach a compromise in its recommendations but the tension that existed then persisted and continues to this day.

One of the manifestations of physician control that health managers must address is corporate practice of medicine legislation. Although many physicians on the committee were concerned about the corporatization of medicine, they ultimately took comfort in occupational control at the state level through state medical societies and licensure authority. At the time, there was also a different antitrust dispensation toward the professions including medicine; antitrust authority applied to commerce, but the professions were considered outside the scope of commercial activity. Physicians, attorneys, engineers, and other professionals were deemed immune from antitrust prosecution. This began to change with the Supreme Court decision in 1943 that ruled against the American Medical Association and in favor of the GHA, an HMO. Subsequent court decisions over several decades removed any ambiguity regarding the applicability of antitrust to healthcare.

The GHA decision was a shot across the bow of organized medicine. Licensure authority was deemed insufficient to maintain occupational control and initiatives were undertaken to garner greater protection from corporatization. Medical interest groups advocated in state capitals for legislation to limit medical decision-making to physicians only. Following the success of their efforts, decisions regarding which forms of care are provided and how they are dispensed became restricted to licensed physicians. Such legislation spread among the states and exists in most of them today. Laws have been amended to enable physician extenders such as nurse practitioners and physician assistants, but they commonly work under the authority of physician oversight.

Nonphysician management has great difficulty in improving productivity when changes threaten physician economic welfare and the modus operandi to which providers are accustomed. So, for example, large-scale and low-cost hospital production for cardiac care or eye care, as occurs in India, has not been embraced in the United States, even though accommodating large numbers of patients at one time contributes to economies of scale and lowers cost structures while maintaining favorable health outcomes. Similarly, there was not much enthusiasm in organized medicine to adopt other technologies disruptive to conventional practices such as electronic medical records or telemedicine. The use of electronic medical records came about largely because of the federal policy established in the wake of the Great Recession and telemedicine across state lines got a boost because of emergency conditions experienced during the COVID epidemic. Most observers expect cost-reducing disruption in healthcare to come from outside the medical establishment but the institution of the corporate practice of medicine remains an impediment to such progress.

An important constraint on provider control is the right of payors, including insurers and consumers, to determine what they will or will not purchase. Consumers are often unaware of their right to say no, but such authority does exist. Insurers are more cognizant of this power and are sometimes willing to exercise it. It greatly facilitates bargaining and helps explain why HMOs and other large organizations can negotiate favorable rates. It also has led to a myriad of authorizations creating bureaucratic aggravation and cost for both providers and consumers.

Conclusion

Occupational control has proliferated in the United States driving up wages and prices, exacerbating income inequality, and undermining productivity-enhancing innovation. It is a major reason American healthcare is so inefficient. There is widespread bipartisan support from the policy establishment for reform, but most of this must occur at the state level. At present, federal appeals for action may be insufficient to move the needle; tougher action, such as conditional Medicare and Medicaid funding, should be considered. Antitrust action is another option, though courts have been reluctant to interfere in state regulation. State governments are often susceptible to interest-group politics and absent widespread public pressure may be loath to effect adequate reform. The national response to the COVID epidemic demonstrates that major innovation can occur in healthcare, and it should encourage policy-makers at all levels of government to act more boldly to reform the institutions of occupational licensure and the corporate practice of medicine.

Chapter 6

Health Insurance

Theory of Insurance

There are important theoretical reasons to have insurance against loss of one kind or another, and a central one involves risk: Most people are averse to risk. Most of us, for example, are more concerned with preserving capital than achieving great wealth, and so we insure ourselves accordingly. Insurance can be expensive, but it can greatly reduce the risk of catastrophic financial loss. Most households would incur a devastating financial setback if their home were destroyed or if they were faced with a large injury-related liability expense. Most would also face significant costs from hospitalization, expensive medication, and extensive specialized physician services. These are generally insurable events, and institutions exist to provide this protection.

Theory holds that consumers are willing to acquire insurance by paying the actuarial costs (cost of occurrence times probability of occurrence) of premiums when they are risk averse, potential losses are significant, and probabilities of occurrence are intermediate. Of course, insurers incur costs too, and these costs are added to actuarial premiums in the price beneficiaries pay. Premiums greater than actuarial cost reduce demand, however, and squeeze out consumers at the margins.

Risk aversion varies from person to person. Some people are more risk tolerant than others and may want higher levels of insurance. Some of the more daring among us may not be very risk averse at all; they embrace risk and are willing to make large bets in the hope of a huge payoff. It is said that this boldness in betting on success is a trait of entrepreneurs. Such persons are less inclined to insure.

DOI: 10.4324/9781003186137-8

Catastrophic losses are relative. A $200,000 hospital bill would be ruinous for most Americans, but not for the top 1% who can easily afford this financial loss. It is not clear that the very wealthy need health and other common forms of insurance, although they particularly benefit from the tax-free nature of employer-sponsored health insurance. The wealthiest among us can self-insure.

Insurable events for the risk averse are defined not only by the potential financial loss relative to one's wealth but also by the likelihood of their occurrence. Automobile insurance is not necessary if one does not drive, but insurance against adverse events where the probability is not zero but very low is another matter. This is a grey area. Malpractice insurance in an occupation where litigation is rare, such as freelance street artist, comes to mind. When the probability of an adverse event is very high, insurance is also problematic. Insurers may be unwilling to offer a product where costs cannot be accurately ascertained and then widely diffused with relatively low premiums. Insurance for homes in wildfire- or hurricane-prone areas comes to mind.

There are also important theoretical reasons why insurance may become inefficient and ineffective. One of them is moral hazard. This concept holds that third-party payment distorts incentives and leads to overconsumption. For example, how many people economize when traveling at company expense? Consumers of healthcare opt for higher levels of utilization and demand top quality when others pay most or all of the bills. And, as we saw in Chapter 4, nonprice competition in healthcare plays a big role in driving up costs. Suppliers compete largely on perceived quality and convenience more than price. Over the long run, this led to a medical arms race in healthcare. Other markets have similar attributes of nonprice competition such as weapons systems and higher education. In these cases, the public sector finances much of the cost either directly or indirectly.

Insurers have options to address moral hazards. Various forms of cost sharing are commonplace in healthcare, and perhaps the most conspicuous of these is the use of deductibles. A deductible requires the beneficiary to pay out-of-pocket up to a prescribed threshold before insurance begins to contribute. This arrangement is attractive theoretically because insurance is meant to protect against catastrophic loss and deductibles are generally well below what most would consider a catastrophic loss. The use of deductibles encourages shopping based on price as well as quality. It also reduces premiums and the burden of paperwork. In effect, beneficiaries are self-insured for amounts below the deductible though they can still take advantage of the negotiated rates as well as the tax benefits of employer-sponsored health insurance. Copayments, a fixed fee, say $30, for use of health services, and coinsurance where the beneficiary pays a percentage of the expense, are also very common forms of cost sharing that help to mitigate moral hazard. Premium sharing, where employees contribute to the cost of policies helps incentivize more efficient insurance choices that in turn can curb excessive utilization.

Moral hazard has an upside. It is argued that there is an externality in the consumption of healthcare, especially for preventive services. This means, for example, that we all benefit from having healthy neighbors who pose little risk of communicable infection and the reassurance that members of our community are looked after. The size of the externality is partly a function of our sense of kinship and that varies within society, rendering agreement about appropriate levels of entitlement problematic. For example, the appetite for social entitlements varies widely between liberals and conservatives.

It may be correct to say that the cost of prevention is justified by the averted future health expenses. This is often true, but not always. For one thing, economic analysis of these decisions must consider the opportunity cost of funds used for prevention. Such funds could be invested and after a long period of time grow to amounts exceeding the cost of care for preventable disease. An important variable is the discount rate. Low rates of return favor prevention compared to high rates because there is less opportunity cost of investing in prevention. Another related problem is that returns from preventive expenditures by healthcare organizations may be realized by Medicare or other insurers, which further reduces incentives for prevention. On the other hand, consumers and employers commonly select insurance plans using the extensiveness of preventive care as an important selling point.

Adverse selection, as described in Chapter 4, is a major issue plaguing health and other insurance markets. Insurers may become overwhelmed with high-cost users and respond with higher premiums, driving out low-cost beneficiaries. This movement, at its starkest, can result in a "death spiral," rendering the line of insurance unsustainable. Insurers seek large groups of beneficiaries to mitigate against this scenario and offer sign-up periods once a year to prevent users from joining only when illness occurs. Such insurers are always striving to improve how they rate and price policies to better reflect risk.

To recap, health insurance both enhances and undermines the well-being of society. It enhances it by mitigating risk for the risk averse but undermines it with moral hazard and adverse selection. Moral hazard is the greater problem over the long run and explains much of the reason American healthcare costs so much. It encourages nonprice competition which, while incentivizing many valuable new technologies, has facilitated an elevated cost structure relative to other developed countries.

Social Insurance

It is important to distinguish between insurance as a general concept and social insurance as a specific one because this is often a point of confusion. Private parties have provided insurance in the marketplace for centuries, and public sectors were not usually involved. This began to change significantly in the 19th century. The concept of social insurance centers on the integration of risk pooling with meeting social entitlements. It evolved first in Europe and then spread globally as insurance provided directly by the public sector or with subsidies in the private sector.

Chapter 2 discussed the evolution of health insurance that emerged in Germany under Otto von Bismarck, which is often considered the birth of modern health insurance. Although healthcare entitlements have expanded in the United States, they have not approximated universal coverage as in other developed nations. Nevertheless, about half of American health expenditures are financed from the public sector, a share that has been growing and is expected to continue to displace the private sector in the foreseeable future. This trend is seen by many as an institutional means to bolster social stability, much as was advocated by Bismarck. The opponents are concerned about the erosion of fundamental American values that center on advancing private property, individualism, and self-sufficiency.

Health Insurance in Practice

Economics as a discipline has deep roots. Minders of mints, even in ancient and medieval times, had a good grasp of the subject. The welfare of workers, and labor economics more generally, has been a topic of interest with a deep literature. But health economics is a relative newcomer. The work of the CCMC was pathbreaking, but relatively little work by economists followed. This changed in the 1960s and 1970s. An important milestone was the work of the Rand Corporation, which was given generous funding to study the demand for healthcare. At the time, policy-makers needed more understanding of price elasticities, for example, important for the design of cost sharing in health insurance policies.

The Rand Corporation designed experiments to observe how consumers respond to different levels of cost sharing. They tested both fee-for-service insurance plans as well as HMOs. Their findings confirmed that the demand for healthcare behaved in a normal fashion with higher out-of-pocket costs driving down utilization. This elasticity, or sensitivity of quantity demanded to price, varied across services. Hospital care was found to be relatively inelastic while chiropractic care and mental health services were much more elastic. Nonurgent visits to the emergency room were an exception to hospital demand and were found to be quite elastic. Demand was also more elastic for the lower-income groups than the higher ones. Physician services and pharmaceuticals were in an intermediate range, while preventive dental care was much more elastic than other dental services. The Rand experiment showed how health expenditures varied as the coinsurance rate went from 95% to zero; expenditures rose as coinsurance fell by about 46%. A large deductible, around $5,300 in 2021 dollars, was also found to be effective at reducing expenditures, by about 31%, compared to an approximation of free care.

The Rand experiment provided evidence that generous coverage of preventive services sharply increases utilization and prevention, particularly for lower-income groups and vulnerable populations such as children. This helps explain why many insurance policies provide first dollar coverage (no deductible) for preventive services such as periodic dental cleaning, primary care prevention visits, and a range of screenings and tests. Yet, at the aggregate level of the entire population, health insurance has not been found to be a very important determinant of the health of beneficiaries. This is not primarily because of health service utilization, but rather because economic development and public health are much more important determinants of population health.

Insurers have fine-tuned the use of cost sharing over the years with more research and changing market conditions. For example, coverage for prescription drugs now commonly uses tiers for generics, preferred branded drugs, other branded drugs, and biologics. Copayments and coinsurance tend to rise respectively for each of these groups, and the impact is to incentivize use of less costly products. This has been effective in managing the utilization of drugs. High levels of cost sharing, for example, have been used for mental health services where demand is relatively elastic. This may be combined with limiting visits based on shrinking marginal benefits as utilization persists.

Profile of Health Insurance Coverage in the United States

Health insurance coverage in the United States is fragmented, with employer-based coverage being the most common type. This is shown in Figure 6.1, which provides data for primary health insurance enumerated by the Kaiser Family Foundation for 2008–2019. Approximately, 158 million people were covered by employers directly or as dependents in 2019. Large federal entitlement programs, primarily Medicaid for lower-income persons and Medicare for those 65 and older as well as some younger than 65 with disabilities, covered another 108 million. Medicaid commonly includes beneficiaries of the Children's Health Insurance Program (CHIP), which was created in the late 1990s after the collapse of the Clinton healthcare reform effort. The CHIP provides funds to states to subsidize healthcare for children of lower- and middle-income families. Some states formally combine CHIP with Medicaid while others do not. The remainder included 29 million uninsured. Figure 6.1 shows the decrease in the number of uninsured

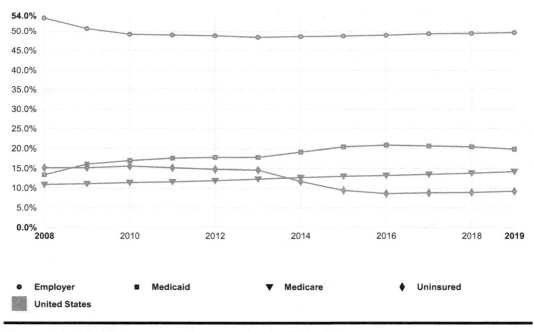

Figure 6.1   Health Insurance Coverage in the United States

Source: www.kff.org/other/state-indicator/total-population/?currentTimeframe=0&sortModel=%7B%22colId%22:%22Location%22,%22sort%22:%22asc%22%7D Health Insurance Coverage of the Total Population, 2019 accessed September 16, 2021.

Reprinted with permission of the Kaiser Family Foundation.

resulting from the implementation of the ACA after 2012. It also shows the corresponding increase in Medicaid coverage.

Not shown are other nongroup insurance that covered 19 million people and the military sector which provided coverage to another 4 million Americans.

Employer-Sponsored Insurance

Employer-sponsored healthcare coverage remains widespread, having been incentivized by tax treatment, wage controls during World War II, union negotiations, and periodic tight labor markets. Employer coverage is typically divided into employee, employee and significant other, and family coverage. Contributions by the employer to that coverage are generally most comprehensive for employee-only, becoming less generous as family members are added. Employers of sufficient size typically offer a choice of insurance plans that may include HMO and non-HMO offerings as well as high-deductible and non-high deductible plans. Preferred provider networks (PPOs) with discounted fee-for-service care are common. Point of Service (POS) plans, intermediate between HMOs and PPOs, are also common. Employer contributions may be most generous for the least-cost options to incentivize economical choice. High-deductible plans, often paired with tax-advantaged health savings accounts, are often encouraged and have gained market share in recent years. Figure 6.2 shows the average total single employee and family premiums for employer-sponsored coverage. High-deductible health plans with savings options have the lowest premiums, but all are high relative to the median household and family household income of $67,521 and $86,372 respectively in 2020.

Medicaid

In its original form, the federal Medicaid program was designed as a safety net for low-income persons. Since then, however, it has evolved into a widespread entitlement for the lower and middle classes. The ACA expanded the eligibility to 138% of the poverty level in most states, which works out to $36,156 for a family of four in 2021. And coverage has recently become even more generous. There are some states, particularly in the South and Midwest, that have not expanded Medicaid despite substantial federal

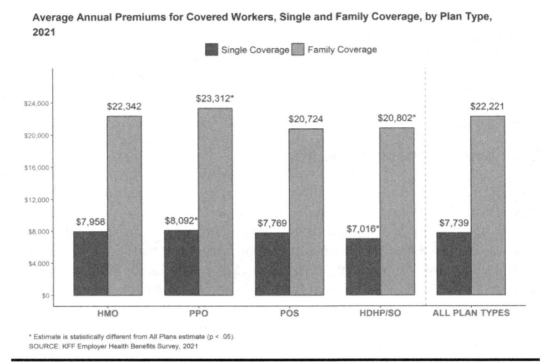

Average Annual Premiums for Covered Workers, Single and Family Coverage, by Plan Type, 2021

* Estimate is statistically different from All Plans estimate (p < .05).
SOURCE: KFF Employer Health Benefits Survey, 2021

Figure 6.2   Employer-Sponsored Health Insurance Premiums

Source: www.kff.org/report-section/ehbs-2020-section-1-cost-of-health-insurance/ 2020 Employer Health Benefits Survey accessed September 13, 2021.

Reprinted with permission of the Kaiser Family Foundation.

incentives associated with the ACA. They have more restrictive criteria for eligibility. But children may be eligible for benefits at higher-income thresholds than adults under CHIP in any state. Increasingly, CHIP funding has been found to crowd out private insurance as employers and families shift children to Medicaid; about 35% of children are enrolled in Medicaid and/ or CHIP. The numbers are higher in some states such as California, where approximately half of children are enrolled.

Medicaid is financed in partnership between federal and state authorities. The federal government provides matching funds of at least 50% for non-ACA-related expenditures. States with lower average personal incomes receive more federal subsidization; for example, Mississippi receives more generous matching funds than Illinois. ACA expansions are largely funded with federal revenues partly supported by increased taxation of upper-income Americans.

The federal government maintains the expectations and standards for Medicaid programs that are implemented by the states. States have flexibility in how they execute federal law, particularly if they receive a federal waiver to deviate from national norms. Under Medicaid, reimbursement rates to providers are generally low and lower than Medicare payments. This has discouraged provider participation and beneficiaries commonly have limited access to providers. Reimbursement rates are often below the average cost of production but may meet marginal costs, and under these conditions, some providers are willing to participate. But low reimbursement rates contribute to system-wide price discrimination, often called cost shifting, where private insurer reimbursement rates are much higher than those for Medicaid and Medicare. Medicaid also relies much more heavily on managed care, with narrow networks and capitation, than other health insurance programs. There, constrained budgets have led to limitations on utilization and services not elsewhere encountered for American health insurance beneficiaries.

It is commonly known that Medicaid covers health services for low- and middle-income persons. Less well-known is that Medicaid finances much of the long-term care for the elderly and disabled in the United States. Figure 6.3 shows that over three quarters of Medicaid enrollment consists of children and adults but over half the expenditures are directed at the disabled and aged. Nursing homes, for example, are quite dependent on the low Medicaid reimbursements they receive for beneficiaries.

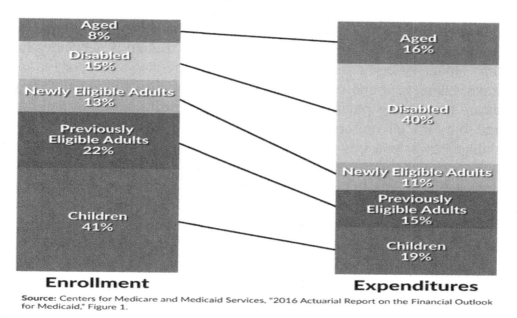

Figure 6.3   Profile of Medicaid Enrollees and Payments

Source: https://www.cms.gov/Research-Statistics-Data-and-Systems/Research/ActuarialStudies/Downloads/MedicaidReport2016.pdf

Medicaid is the low-cost sector of US healthcare. It is a bargain for the taxpayer because of low reimbursement rates and parsimonious utilization. But it imposes constraints on the lower-income Americans who use it that are unknown to those with higher incomes. Thus far, this disparity has been socially acceptable. Lower-income Americans are not as well organized as the well-off and have not advanced this issue to serious bipartisan national debate.

Medicare

Medicare, in the United States, was originally designed to cover those 65 and older and eligible for social security. Since its inception, the program has been expanded to cover segments of the under-65 population including those with kidney failure and other disabilities established by the Social Security Administration. It is divided into four major programs with the two oldest, Parts A and B, established at the outset in 1965. Part A covers inpatient services and is financed primarily through social security contributions. It is backed by a designated Part A trust fund. Most Part A recipients gain coverage as they gain social security eligibility after 10 years of employment or through a spousal relationship. It is possible to buy in, however. Inpatient coverage has limitations based on spells of illness, which is defined as the time from hospital admission to 60 days after discharge without readmission. Medicare limits hospital payment beyond 90 days, though beneficiaries have lifetime limited reserves that can be used. There are also restrictions to inpatient psychiatric care and physical, occupational, or speech therapy services. Medicare Part A does pay for skilled nursing home care upon hospital discharge, but for a circumscribed period.

Unlike Part A, which is near universal, Part B, which covers physician services, is optional and beneficiaries must enroll in it. Most do because while cost sharing is greater than Part A, it is heavily subsidized by the federal government, which finances most of it. Beneficiaries pay premiums that are progressive; that is to say, higher-income beneficiaries pay more. The program has deductibles and coinsurance, the latter commonly set at 20%. Part B also covers durable medical equipment, laboratory and diagnostic tests, outpatient hospital services, home health, and other forms of care. Federal financing is not associated with a social security trust fund but rather with a supplemental fund supported by general revenues.

Medicare Part C is a comprehensive program housing Parts A, B, and D. Part D was established with the Medicare Modernization Act of 2003 and implemented in 2006. A primary objective of this legislation was the provision of a Medicare prescription drug benefit, as no such benefit then existed, except in the context of hospitalization, and pharmacy benefits had become widespread in private insurance policies. Part D is financed much like Part B with premiums paid by beneficiaries and most of the cost financed by federal general revenues channeled to a supplemental Medicare trust fund. Part D was designed to promote competition among plans that compete for Medicare enrollees. The plans are generally private but there is a fallback public option for regions without access to adequate private provision.

Medicare Part C, known as Medicare Advantage, provides comprehensive care for inpatient, outpatient, prescription drugs and other healthcare services such as vision or dental care. Beneficiaries commonly select from different managed care options including HMOs and PPOs. Under Medicare Advantage, the choice of providers is usually narrower than in traditional Medicare but cost sharing and covered services are more generous. These integrated systems offer quality advantages with better coordination of care and comprehensive health information systems. But they may not provide access to all subspecialists or the most highly ranked providers. Medicare Advantage has been popular, gaining market share relative to traditional Medicare with 42% of the market in 2021. There is considerable regional variation with 52% in Minnesota, 51% in Florida, and 49% participation in Hawaii (80% in Puerto Rico) but only 4% in sparsely populated Wyoming and only 1% in Alaska.

Enrollment in Medicare Advantage also obviates the need for Medigap policies. These supplemental policies, used by many enrolled in traditional Medicare, are available in defined packages and cover cost sharing and gaps within basic Medicare coverage. Medigap options vary in coverage of international travel, long-term care, and cost-sharing choices.

The solvency of the trust fund for Medicare Part A is a matter of looming fiscal concern. Expenditures have exceeded revenues for some time and the best models indicate exhaustion in the near term. This depletion will render Medicare Part A completely dependent on ongoing revenues. The various reasons for growing Medicare insolvency include, notably, the retirement of baby boomers, who both move into Medicare and stop paying social security taxes into the fund. Rising prices along with technology-induced increases in utilization are also factors. Figure 6.4 shows Medicare trust fund exhaustion in 2026. A more pessimistic variant has exhaustion occurring in 2024. In either case, policy-makers must address this issue soon unless more optimistic scenarios prevail. The options include increasing social security taxes, reducing benefits, or cutting reimbursements. These

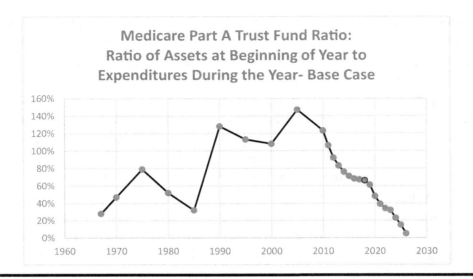

Figure 6.4   Depletion of Medicare Part A Trust Fund

Source: **https://www.cms.gov/files/document/2021-medicare-trustees-report.pdf**

alternatives are unpopular with constituents and problematic for Washington. The Supplementary Medical Trust Fund is not currently at risk of depletion, but it does contribute to the wider macroeconomic problem of rising budget deficits and debt. An alternative approach to exhaustion of Part A is merging with Part B. This is convenient from a political standpoint but will further deepen the fiscal deficit and debt.

Military Healthcare

Military healthcare which can be defined to include care provided by the armed services as well as the Department of Veterans Affairs (VA), was the primary source of healthcare finance for over 4 million persons in 2019. Many military beneficiaries use non-VA forms of health insurance as their primary payer. Military beneficiaries include active-duty personnel, dependents, and retirees. Care may be provided directly in military-operated facilities or through the civilian sector as part of a three-service coordinated program known as Tricare. The VA operates a nationwide network of hospitals and healthcare facilities serving veterans. Prioritization in those facilities is given to those with service-related injuries and disabilities. The military sector has the dual functions of wartime preparedness and more routine peacetime care, and it must meet the demand for both with budgeted finance. This imposes constraints that can lead to nonprice rationing.

Nongroup

Nongroup health insurance enrollees are those who obtain health insurance on an individual or family basis without access to employer-sponsored coverage or publicly provided programs. This category includes those in the small business sector and early retirees. Health insurance exchanges created by the ACA serve as a vehicle for a large segment of this group. These exchanges generally provide subsidies to those ineligible for Medicaid and are considered a middle-class entitlement. Exchanges created by the ACA enrolled about 12 million people in 2021. In addition, there are private exchanges that cater to individuals and small businesses; individuals can also enroll in managed care plans or other forms of health insurance outside of exchange mechanisms. Collectively, nongroup plans accounted for the health insurance of 19 million Americans in 2019.

The Uninsured

The United States has higher levels of uninsured citizens than other developed countries, and it is a matter of some concern. This lack of health insurance is concentrated in certain sectors of the population including Hispanics, immigrants, and those living in the southern states where Medicaid expansions have not become the norm. It also includes those in occupations such as in agriculture, construction, low-wage services, and the arts; low-wage workers and the young in particular are overrepresented among the uninsured. Some economists argue that the lack of insurance among the young and healthy is a rational response to the extraordinarily high cost of health insurance and the risks they face. But others argue that a developed society such as ours should provide coverage for all as a matter of national policy. The ACA significantly moved the United States toward universal coverage. The number of uninsured was estimated at approximately 31 million in 2020.

Long-Term Care Insurance

Coverage for long-term care, which includes skilled nursing homes and home healthcare is often very limited or nonexistent in employer-provided medical insurance. Employers commonly provide dental and vision insurance to employees but rarely pay for long-term care insurance. Many Americans believe Medicare covers this, but, in fact, coverage can be limited to just a few months after discharge from a hospital. Medicaid does provide extended long-term care coverage but only once a beneficiary's assets have been largely depleted for a period of five years. The look-back period of five years is designed to protect taxpayers from fraud by reducing the wealth transfers a beneficiary can make to children to gain eligibility. In some respects, Medicaid offers long-term care coverage with a large deductible, one amounting to most of your assets. For a large proportion of Americans, this is not an insurmountable problem because their asset levels are low; for them Medicaid is the provider of long-term care insurance. The wealthy on the other hand can self-insure. Those with millions of dollars in assets can generally afford a few years in a nursing home at a $100,000 or more annual expense. Home care and assisted living tend to be less costly.

There is a segment of the population in the middle class that is ill pre-pared for long-term care, however. Their assets are too high for Medicaid eligibility, and they do not have enough wealth to self-insure. For these people, private long-term care insurance is available. This market is troubled, however; insurers have experienced adverse selection and they have under-estimated the costs of long-term care expenses. Beneficiaries are living lon-ger and incurring higher expenses. Moreover, insurers have underperformed in financial markets with a long period of exceptionally low interest rates. Consumers of long-term care coverage commonly find unattractive terms that may not include adjustments for inflation but may include the termina-tion of benefits for a missed payment. In any event, premiums are high and deter many shoppers who are quite sensitive to prices in this market; they commonly fall back on family as their effective long-term care policy. Some states have explored mixed private–public long-term care programs where beneficiaries purchase some limited private insurance, perhaps with infla-tion protection, in return for asset protection if they fall back on Medicaid. California has such a plan called the California Partnership for Long Term Care. Technology has helped too. Medical interventions such as hip replace-ments and remote sensing help keep more of the aged and the infirm at home and out of nursing facilities. Growth in long-term care has been con-centrated in more affordable home healthcare and assisted living facilities.

Health Insurance Coverage Going Forward

Going forward, several issues regarding health insurance are a concern. First, the problem of the uninsured continues to vex us; the progressive goal of universal coverage remains unfulfilled. With over 30 million uninsured in the United States, about 9% of the population, many of those progressives believe we are not getting any closer to universal coverage and that more insurance expansion is necessary. Many of the states that opted to forgo Medicaid expansion may yet succumb to federal financial incentives, however; with renewed outreach Medicaid enrollment may rise again. Expansion of exchange subsidies is expected to further boost enrollment, and other measures may be forthcoming. More aggressive measures include Medicare-for-All proposals, which opponents fiercely resist, fearing, among other things, that such measures would ultimately result in something closer to Medicaid-for-All as budget pressures mount. A single-payer system such as Medicare-for-All is politically more difficult to achieve than establishing a public option where consumers not eligible for Medicare or Medicaid choose between private and publicly provided insurance. Some states are already laying out such a path. Public options are likely to be lower cost than private options, with lower reimbursement rates to providers and lower administrative costs. Over time, such plans can be expected to displace many in the private sector as consumers switch to more affordable plans. It is not surprising that this scenario is not popular with providers, insurers, or suppliers who fear for their financial well-being.

Budget solvency for federal programs is another top concern. As noted, the Medicare Part A trust fund will soon be depleted in most analyses, and the old-age social security fund is projected to exhaust in the 2030s. Much of the problem is demographic, with fewer younger workers to support greater numbers of older social security and Medicare beneficiaries. Life expectancy has been on the rise, and most can expect to live well past 65, especially those from the higher-income strata. Figure 6.5 shows how the number of workers per Medicare beneficiary will fall from over 4 in 1981 to a projected 2.3 in 2041. The ratio for the social security old age fund is projected to be 2.2 workers per beneficiary by 2041.

The third problem to emphasize is the cost of healthcare. Production costs are too high, shielded by third-party payment and an environment of monopolistic competition. The shift toward high deductible plans helps to elevate the role of price in consumer choice, but many economists argue that more needs to be done. Tax treatment of insurance is a topic of some bipartisan agreement among economists. Eliminating, or at least curbing, the tax exemption of health insurance as envisioned, but never implemented with the Cadillac tax in the ACA, was a laudable effort. A variant of this should be resurrected. It will lead to greater efficiency in healthcare and generate considerable tax revenue to address widening budget gaps.

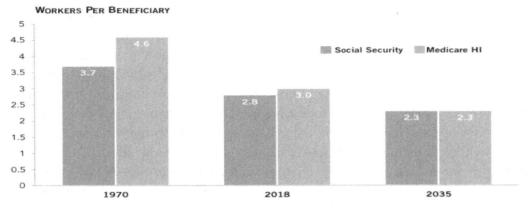

SOURCE: Social Security Administration. *The 2019 Annual Report of the Board of Trustees of the Federal Old-Age and Survivors Insurance and Federal Disability Insurance Trust Funds,* April 2019, and Centers for Medicare and Medicaid Services, *2019 Annual Report of the Boards of Trustees of the Federal Hospital Insurance and Federal Supplementary Medical Insurance Trust Funds,* April 2019. Compiled by PGPF.

© 2019 Peter G. Peterson Foundation

PGPF.ORG

Figure 6.5   Workers per Social Security Beneficiary

Source: https://www.pgpf.org/blog/2021/09/five-charts-about-the-future-of-social-security-and-medicare

Reprinted with permission of the Peter G. Peterson Foundation.

Perhaps, of even greater importance is the lack of sufficient mechanisms to forgo health expenditures when benefits do not justify costs. How much is too much, and how do we best determine what not to provide? There are opportunity costs to resource allocation to the health sector; resources could be used elsewhere, and such decision-making impacts allocative efficiency. This is the subject of Chapter 7.

Allocative Efficiency and Cost-Effectiveness Analysis

Efficiency Defined

Efficiency is a concept central to economics. It has driven humanity's incredible spread of wealth over the last two centuries, and our prosperity and well-being depend on it. But the term is not well understood. Efficiency means different things to different people. For example, an engineer when asked about efficiency may refer to the relationship between inputs and output in production. The engineer, as a rule, will seek more output for a given supply of inputs. This is higher productivity assuming there is no change in the quality of output. Economists sometimes call this technical efficiency. It is an important and key driver of long-run economic growth.

Managers and economists look beyond technical efficiency in decisions about which technology to select. Input prices are important too because ultimately low-cost production is a key objective. A more labor-intensive technology may be preferable to a capital-intensive one if low labor costs offset the higher costs of new, but expensive capital-intensive production or perhaps different conditions prevail, and capital-intensive production is the better choice. The use of the least-cost technology, with quality held constant, is often termed productive efficiency. Efficient production optimizes between available technologies and input prices. Theory also assumes profit maximization will incentivize least-cost production as producers compete on price. In practice, as noted earlier, incentives and market conditions may be insufficient to ensure efficient production and X-inefficiency may set in with too many or overpaid inputs.

DOI: 10.4324/9781003186137-9

Managers and economists are not always on the same page and may part ways on the meaning of "efficiency." Managers are focused on competitive costs and have relatively little interest in the economy-wide allocation of goods and services. Economists, in contrast, have a keen interest in both efficient production and allocation within society. Allocative efficiency entails ensuring that resources are distributed to optimize social welfare; expenditures should be allocated to generate the greatest level of satisfaction possible per dollar spent. All mutually beneficial transactions between buyers and sellers should occur and resources should generate the greatest net social gains for a given distribution of income and wealth.

Decisions must be made about how best to spend resources, and efficient production is an insufficient reason. For example, a university could identify the least-cost method of a field trip to outer space. But such an extravagance, even with the least-cost choice of space flight, might not be efficient because there is the opportunity cost of funds used for this expense. Money for the field trip could instead be allocated to new laboratories or classrooms; it could be used to hire more faculty for more courses, or tuition could be cut so families and students have greater resources to use at their discretion.

One important caveat about allocative efficiency should be noted: Theory assumes a given distribution of income and wealth in determining efficient resource allocation. Many observers readily concede the status quo is not necessarily equitable or fair. Some economists—Karl Marx comes to mind—have prioritized equity in their paradigms. Marxists believe unjust resource allocation threatens the capitalist order in the long run. Of course, capitalist countries have evolved social safety nets to help assuage human suffering and social instability. Healthcare and education are accorded a special status by the International Monetary Fund and World Bank as critical sectors where publicly provided entitlements are endorsed as a matter of justice, social stability, and investment in productive capacity. Yet many countries have tiered healthcare systems with better care for the more affluent, just as the well-to-do in those countries receive better goods and services across the board. Is this just? Is it inevitable? These are important questions with great bearing on allocative efficiency in the United States and around the world.

One of the unique characteristics of the American health sector is a reluctance to embrace allocative efficiency with any transparent implementation. In most sectors of the economy, consumers and households make routine decisions about how to allocate their budget to the best effect. Decisions are made about how much is too much when purchasing housing, automobiles, or vacations. Levels of income and wealth are important determinants as are tastes and preferences. Healthcare has moved in this direction to some extent as high deductible plans, many with health savings accounts or similar savings vehicles, have become more widespread. But much of healthcare is covered by insurers, both public and private, where such decision-making is opaque at best.

Americans struggle with the ethics of allocating resources away from health when costs are high. Insurers are loath to identify how much is too much, especially in a transparent manner. To some extent, the public sector leads the way in coverage decisions, but Medicare does not embrace cost-effectiveness analysis in its deliberations over coverage decisions. Few politicians want to be identified with policies that could curtail the health of anyone. Consumers, subject to moral hazard and protected from prices, are inclined to overconsume healthcare, opting for limitless levels of expenditure to preserve and improve their health. Yet society cannot afford to provide everyone with everything an evolving medical technology can deliver.

This issue of allocative efficiency was uncomfortably brought into public view during the COVID-19 epidemic. For many Americans, there were important and difficult tradeoffs between lives and livelihoods. Many, particularly on the more progressive end of the political spectrum, gave more weight to protecting lives than did many in the business community, who sometimes appeared more concerned about the economy; and the result was partisan conflict. The media emphasized health impacts and provided saturation coverage of the expert analysis and recommendations from the medical and public health communities with relatively little input from economists and the business community.

The health professions sometimes regard allocative efficiency as unethical based on their primary commitment to saving lives and promoting health. They commonly seek to maximize health rather than optimize by weighing costs and benefits. The slighting of cost considerations in the provision of healthcare raises an ethical issue; in the United States, it has been a roadblock to developing mechanisms to improve allocative efficiency. It helps explain the problematic nature of tradeoffs, even as the declared ethics of the health professions has led to an avoidance of such difficult discussions. We can be certain that expensive new health technologies will continue to evolve. The next pandemic will require tradeoffs of economic and social activity with the imperatives of healthcare. No doubt we will continue to need leadership on this issue. How will we decide where to draw the line? Who will do this and how transparent will such decisions be?

Overview of Cost-Effectiveness Analysis

A common approach to determining how much healthcare is too much is the use of cost-effectiveness analysis. It provides a more formal means of assessing how best to allocate limited budgets than the calculation commonly used by households and businesses. Limited resources can be allocated to those expenditures that generate the greatest "bang for the buck," or put another way, that generate the greatest improvements in health per dollar spent. Cost-effectiveness analysis is broadly used in other countries to help guide coverage decisions. It is not the only type of criteria used, but it is an important one. The United Kingdom, Australia, Canada, the Netherlands, and Germany, for example, make significant use of cost-effectiveness analysis in healthcare. Public and private insurers in the United States are more reluctant to embrace this explicit type of analysis that puts a dollar value on health and life itself. Medicare policy-makers, for example, avoid explicit use of cost-effectiveness analysis in the United States; others, however, are pressing forward with research and analysis. Teams of physicians, economists, and others publish important analyses in academic journals, and nonacademic organizations such as the Institute for Clinical and Economic Review (ICER) are major contributors to understanding these issues. Insurers, employers, households, and others can use this work. Although the pharmaceutical or medical device industries provide cost-effectiveness information at times, users should be careful and recognize biases. Results can be misleading.

Methods of Cost-Effectiveness Analysis

Cost-effectiveness analysis entails comparison of two or more healthcare interventions. They could be preventive, diagnostic, or treatment oriented. Such studies commonly involve comparing a new technology to the status quo; new drugs, screening tests, or medical devices are typical subjects of such studies. Researchers must measure and compare the costs of interventions as well as the effects, which are usually measured in terms of changes to health. An analysis that measures both costs and effects in dollars is called a cost–benefit analysis. Usually though, effects are measured in health outcomes such as less pain, more mobility, improved diagnostic accuracy, or longer life. Studies that measure outcomes in terms of improved life expectancy or quality-adjusted life expectancy are often called cost-utility analyses. A variant, used commonly in global settings, employs disability-adjusted life years. Quality and disability-adjusted life years weight a year of life by health impairment. Perfect health would be weighted with a one. Serious impairments, such as dementia or paralysis, however, are weighted much lower, though are usually greater than zero.

Cost-effectiveness analysis sometimes provides clear evidence that a new technology is an improvement to efficiency, which means it both improves health and costs less. In contrast, a new technology is clearly inefficient if it both undermines health and costs more. Unfortunately, many new technologies are ambiguous in their capabilities, either improving health but at greater cost or reducing costs but with adverse health impacts. Figure 7.1 shows the possible outcomes of cost-effectiveness analysis. Quadrant IV is clearly more efficient as it leads to cost savings and better health. Quadrant I is clearly less efficient; new technology that costs more and undermines health should be avoided. But quadrants II and III are ambiguous. These cases must be evaluated to compare changes in health outcomes as well as cost. For example, a substantial improvement in health at very low cost is likely to be cost-effective.

An advantage of cost-utility analysis is a common denominator such as cost per quality-adjusted life year. Findings can be compared across a wide range of healthcare interventions. Policy-makers and societies more generally can then choose a threshold of how many dollars they are willing to allocate for a quality or disability-adjusted life year. More affluent countries can and do use higher thresholds. The United States does not have an official government-sanctioned level, but the ICER threshold of approximately $150,000 per quality-adjusted life year has become something of a proxy that has gained acceptance. The most generous countries range from $100,000 to $200,000 per quality-adjusted life year. Most countries employing this

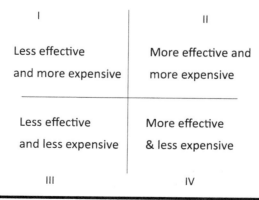

Figure 7.1 Cost-Effectiveness Matrix

approach, including Canada, the Netherlands, Japan, and Australia, had thresholds of under $100,000 per quality-adjusted life year according to the *Wall Street Journal* in 2019. The UK was on the low end among developed countries at under $50,000 per quality-adjusted life year.

Industry has an incentive to develop new technologies treating common ailments where an effective innovation can become a blockbuster generating a large volume of sales. Economies of scale helps spread substantial research and development costs to lower the average cost. This helps with affordable pricing. Treatments for rare diseases tend to generate less interest in the pharmaceutical industry if large development costs are spread among relatively few buyers. Prices tend to be high in this case and less likely to clear cost-effectiveness thresholds. Figure 7.2 shows patient costs declining with greater use of new and costly prescription medications. The cost of Carbaglu for treating ammonia in blood at $300,000 per year far exceeds the roughly $50,000 per year for more widely used Tracleer, a drug for pulmonary hypertension. Busilvex, a leukemia medication is even less costly despite being less commonly used than Tracleer. Rare disease treatments with low levels of volume and adverse cost structure may require special incentives to develop "orphan" drugs.

Analysts who consider where new technology can be most helpful on a population basis look at the impact of disease in terms of premature death as well as disability and impaired quality of life. Some conditions such as

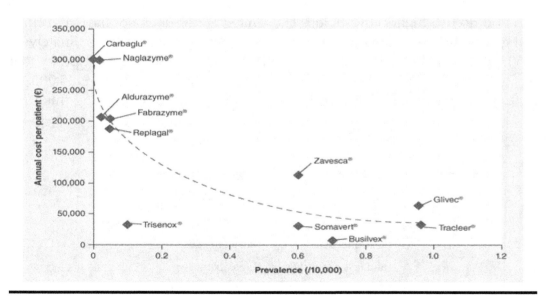

Figure 7.2   Economies of Scale in Prescription Drugs

Source: https://www.futuremedicine.com/doi/full/10.2217/cer.14.34

Reprinted with permission of Future Medicine.

Age-standardized disability adjusted life year (DALY) rate per 100,000 population, by disease, 2019

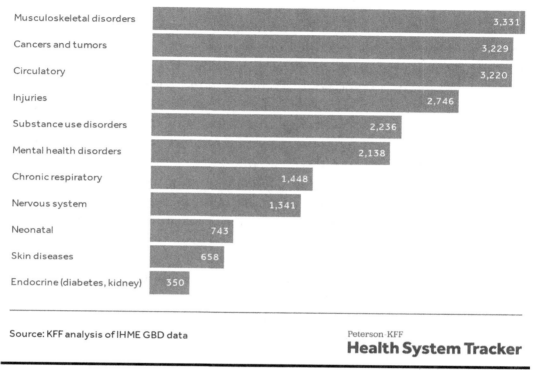

Source: KFF analysis of IHME GBD data

Peterson-KFF
Health System Tracker

Figure 7.3 Mortality and Morbidity for Common Illness

Source: https://www.healthsystemtracker.org/indicator/health-well-being/disability-adjusted-life-years/ accessed September 13, 2021

Reprinted with permission of the Peterson-Kaiser Health System Tracker.

heart disease, cardiac arrest, and lung cancer primarily impact years of life lost (mortality), while others such as back and neck pain, skin disease, and depression largely impact the quality of life measured by years lived with disability (morbidity). Both mortality and morbidity are costly to the health of a population and accordingly they flag large potential markets for improved intervention. Figure 7.3 shows how both of these impact disability-adjusted life years. Musculoskeletal problems exceed cancer in terms of disability-adjusted life years because of their widespread prevalence.

Discounting and Distribution

One of the more controversial aspects of cost-effectiveness analysis is the use of discounting. A key component of financial theory involves the time value of money. The theory holds that people save more when interest rates are higher. They defer spending and associated gratification now for future spending. The time value of money is measured by interest rates. The higher the rate, the greater the premium on the present relative to the future. Interest rates are complicated and measure other things as well including the marginal productivity of capital. But few in finance and economics doubt the importance of discounting future costs and revenues to account for the time value of money. Money flows in the future should be discounted to reflect the opportunity cost of investing. Money makes money over time. Lower rates of return as measured by interest rates, or discount rates more generally, improve the economic viability of long-term preventive interventions. For example, the present value of averting cancer-related costs decades into the future is greater when discount rates are lower. There are fewer alternative uses for funds when interest rates are low. Another facet of discounting is the discounting of health itself. This too is controversial, but analysis often discounts health as well as money. In practice, many people show a great deal of indifference to their future health, behaving in ways that bring immediate gratification while jeopardizing future well-being.

The distribution of costs and outcomes is also an important aspect of cost-effectiveness analysis, and studies should indicate any distributional impact. Shifting from one technology to another commonly entails costs. But to whom? For example, a new technology may impact access to healthcare for different segments of the population or it may impact the cost of production for some more than others. Similarly, the use of a different technology may have differential health outcomes within the population. Analysts need to be cognizant of the distributional dimension, particularly when those adversely affected are not well organized and whose voices, accordingly, may well be muted. In our politically charged world, policy making and coverage decisions may be more sensitive to distributional issues than efficiency.

Cost-Effectiveness Analysis in Practice

Cost-effectiveness analysis can help payers generate the greatest health with limited resources. A wide range of very cost-effective technologies is now available, and they should be prioritized. Some are even cost-saving such as immunizations for children. Public health measures are often quite efficient, such as the establishment of clean water and sanitation systems. To be sure, these measures occasionally meet resistance. Families may refuse to immunize children for fear of side effects, real or imagined. Fluoridation of water to prevent tooth decay is another case in point: It has been found to be very cost-effective, even cost-saving, as the expense of water fluoridation is more than offset by reduced dental costs; yet in many communities, vocal opposition has objected to the very idea of government authority introducing such additives to the water supply. Some have raised concerns about side effects such as fluorosis, which is caused by an overexposure to fluoride. They also argue that individuals can obtain fluoride readily from toothpaste or mouthwash or receive applications during dental care.

Medical interventions often have higher costs relative to benefits compared to many public health interventions. But health technologies that confer large benefits often meet the thresholds of cost-effectiveness, and new technologies can be cost-effective, even if expensive at first glance. Take the routine hip replacement, the cost of which commonly exceeds 30,000 dollars. This procedure is usually provided to older patients, often in their 80s and 90s, and one might think limited years of life expectancy would preclude findings of cost-effectiveness. In fact, the procedure is so successful in keeping older persons out of costly care homes and improving the quality of life that it is highly recommended, even for very elderly patients. The same can be said for a variety of heart-related procedures. They may be costly, but they have a substantial impact on both additional years of life and quality of life.

The need for greater use of cost-effectiveness studies has been strengthened by the wave of new and costly biological drugs that have emerged in recent decades. For example, biologics are derived from tissue cultures, are often administered by infusion or injection, and are generally much more costly to develop and produce than more traditional pills or capsules. Some of these drugs have been remarkably effective. The treatment for Hepatitis C is a case in point. Previously, Hepatitis C was difficult to cure and could lead to serious liver disease and even death. When Sovaldi, a breakthrough curative drug was launched in late 2013 and 2014, the problem of its high cost immediately emerged. Many patients with Hepatitis C are of the low-income category and receive publicly provided and budgeted health insurance. As a result, insurers and providers began to triage, providing the medication to those most in need. This problem was not confined to the United States. Figure 7.4, created by the Canadian Agency for Drugs and Technologies in Health (CADTH) and Indigenous Services Canada, shows analysis for a segment of the population with Hepatitis C. The use of Sovaldi, or any of the other drugs that soon emerged for Hepatitis C, adds substantial cost to treatment. But they also add several quality-adjusted life years so that the cost per additional quality-adjusted life year with use of these drugs falls in an acceptable range. An eight-week course of Harvoni emerged as a leading

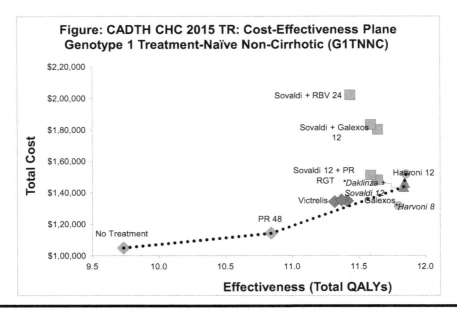

Figure 7.4   Cost-Effectiveness Analysis of Treatment Options for Hepatitis C

Source: https://cadth.ca/drugs-chronic-hepatitis-c-infection

https://cadth.ca/sites/default/files/pdf/TR0008_Cost-Effectiveness_Report.pdf

Reprinted with permission of the Canadian Agency for Drugs and Technologies in Health and Indigenous Services Canada.

choice in this analysis based on retail prices because it provided a favorable profile of added costs and improved health relative to other options. But researchers estimated that it would cost about 1% of Canada's GDP to treat all those with Hepatitis C in the country. This will likely limit allocation to those most in need for the foreseeable future.

The National Institute for Health and Care Excellence (NICE)

The United Kingdom (UK) has been a leader in the use of cost-effectiveness analysis. Its National Health Service (NHS) both finances and provides care for most residents of the UK. It largely budgets healthcare resources and it must make decisions about what it can and cannot afford. The National Institute for Health and Care Excellence (NICE) collects and provides research used for coverage recommendations by the NHS. The NHS provides recommended technologies but there is often latitude in the implementation that local authorities control. And not all technologies have been evaluated, which encourages more local autonomy. Plainly, cost-effectiveness is an important criterion for recommendation. The UK uses a substantially lower threshold of cost per quality-adjusted life year than the United States and many other developed countries. Moreover, cost-effectiveness is not the only determinant as NICE also considers budget impacts; medical innovations affecting widespread health conditions can have large budget impacts. So, for example, while NICE found the use of Entresto for heart failure to be cost-effective, limitations were placed on its use, channeling the drug to only those with more advanced health failure. NICE also considers if a new technology is novel or simply a modified variant of something that now exists and if it addresses an unmet need. In addition, the cost per quality-adjusted threshold is not rigid; thresholds can be raised in a special dispensation for relatively rare conditions.

For many conditions, there may be several competing technologies with some better suited to different subgroups of the population. Medicine is moving away from one size fits all, for example, and toward more personalized care based on genetic and other characteristics of the individual. The complexity of decision-making is increasing, and no doubt it will come to depend on artificial intelligence to help guide medical and other health decisions. Personalized medicine is in its infancy and has yet to fully impact the use of cost-effectiveness analysis.

Conclusion

Economics concerns the allocation of scarce resources. So long as scarcity exists, there will be opportunity costs of allocating resources to healthcare. When the economy is fully employed and tradeoffs exist about what is produced, the more money we invest in health-related matters the less is available for other sectors such as education, leisure, and the arts. Going forward, this will require difficult choices.

Resources must be rationed, and market systems ordinarily rely on income and prices to do this. In healthcare, third-party insurance drives a wedge between price and cost, unlike other sectors of the economy. Insurers are called upon to make such decisions but when they balk at rendering tough decisions, they undermine allocative efficiency. The use of cost-effectiveness analysis can help cut through the confusion, assist decision makers, and improve allocative efficiency. To some extent, the United States uses nonmonetary costs to ration; inconveniences such as waiting times or bureaucracy have been shown to be important costs, especially for the insured. This kind of rationing tends to be more prevalent in under-resourced and budgeted public health insurance programs such as Medicaid or programs for veterans. Cost-effectiveness analysis should take these costs into account as well.

More widespread use of the cost-effectiveness analysis will require a greater degree of courage, particularly by our political leaders, to bring the United States more into line with international practice. Resistance by industry is another big obstacle. Monopolistic competition is characterized by product and service differentiation that sometimes delivers real improvement; nevertheless, often similar products rely more on the perception of improvement than fact. Suppliers of this variety of products or services do not wish to fall prey to the systematic analysis of incremental costs and benefits. If they resist, they can be an effective voice in our pluralistic democracy. These political forces are powerful, and perhaps conditions must get worse before America more fully and gradually integrates cost-effectiveness analysis into the fabric of the health sector.

In conclusion, economic theory and specifically notions of productive and allocative efficiency provide economists with a view of efficiency at a given point in time. It is important. But of greater importance over time is another concept commonly termed dynamic efficiency. This refers to the ability of an economy to adopt new and better production including the use of new technology and improved management. It depends critically on the innovative spirit of the population and institutions to accommodate change. The American health sector, while no paragon of virtue, does excel in one respect, and that is new technology. It stands out in the world as a driving force in developing new drugs, devices, and other medical technologies. Dynamic efficiency and the role of technological advancement in healthcare is our next topic and much of the focus of Section III.

THE HEALTH SECTOR, MACROECONOMICS, AND ECONOMIC DEVELOPMENT

Chapter 8

Production and Productivity in the Health Sector

Introduction: Technology and Productivity

The health sector is a part of the wider economy, albeit a large and growing one, and its output combines with other parts of the economy to improve our well-being. Our population and affluence have grown along with the productivity of the economy, and that productivity, especially labor, is the key economic variable driving prosperity. The human population may level-off or even decline, by design or default, but our overall affluence is likely to increase going forward. This chapter explores the concept of productivity and how it evolved in the production of both health and health services.

Chapter 7 introduced the notion of engineering efficiency: the physical relationship between inputs and outputs. The greater the output for a given level of input, the greater the engineering efficiency. Output per worker also greatly concerns economists. Increases in output per worker are known as labor productivity improvements. If we consider an example of this from history, the Neolithic Revolution around 10,000 BC signaled a transition of many societies from hunter-gatherers to farmers and herdsmen, facilitating greater levels of food output and, in turn, larger, more settled populations; such communities could then engage in a wide range of economic activities. Figure 8.1 shows the takeoff in human population following the Neolithic Revolution based on the estimates of various scholars. The scale is logarithmic, a scale that better captures the rates of change. The impact of this

DOI: 10.4324/9781003186137-11

Historical Human Populations

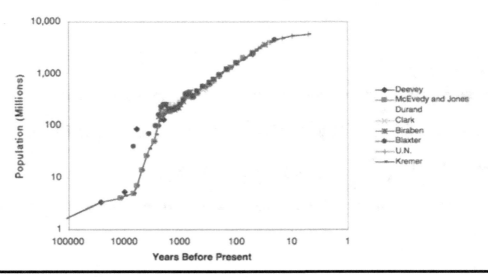

Figure 8.1   Neolithic Revolution and Population Growth

Source: https://equitablegrowth.org/estimates-world-gdp-one-million-b-c-present-1998-view-1998-honest-broker-week-may-24-2014-2/

Reprinted with permission of the Washington Center for Equitable Growth.

transition on quality of life has been the subject of debate, with some scholars noting that the growth of population often offset the growth of output; for much of the population, it is not clear that their lives were better than those of their hunter-gatherer ancestors. But those individuals in positions of power—elites—no doubt enjoyed a higher standard of material affluence than the common field hand.

The advent of planting, irrigating, and harvesting crops such as wheat and barley was a revolution in technology, and the same can be said for the introduction of herding livestock such as sheep, goats, pigs, and cattle. This agricultural revolution eventually spread to most corners of the world, fueling population growth and environmental transformation. But the transition from the old ways to the new brought discontinuity. It transformed societies, eventually establishing a new normal. It showed that in the long run it is technology that is the primary driver of the relationship between inputs and output. Technical changes to improve labor productivity were marginal for millennia after the Neolithic Revolution and even as late as the years just prior to the Industrial Revolution. Then, commencing in the 18th and 19th centuries, a host of innovations, notably the use of steam power, were introduced. This transition catalyzed labor productivity and increased the contribution of labor to the value of output, which then drove higher labor compensation in the United Kingdom, the United States, and around the world.

The Production Function

The relationship between input and output can be described with production functions specifying inputs, usually labor and capital, but sometimes also including entrepreneurship or natural resources such as land. These models show how increased levels of capital (machines) or other inputs per worker tend to increase output and labor productivity. They also show the importance of the quality of capital and embodied technology. This is often more important than the quantity of capital, particularly in the long run. The quality of labor is also of great importance; new technology often requires highly educated workers, and a key dimension of labor quality is the workforce's level of education.

Production functions have been developed for the health sector. Healthcare tends to be labor intensive, with many care providers and staff; here, production requires large numbers of workers relative to other inputs. In this setting, labor can be measured in terms of full-time equivalents. Filling out the setting, other inputs include buildings and utilities, equipment, and supplies. The output is health, restored or improved, but measuring it is problematic, as noted in our discussion of cost-effectiveness analysis. Measures of mortality or death rates are relatively easy to use in production research. Life expectancy, cause of death, infant mortality, or under-age-5 mortality are all common measures. Morbidity, which refers to disease, injury, or disability, provides an alternative source of measures. The rate of new cases of a disease or ailment in a population, called incidence, is a common measure as is the total rate of cases in a population known as prevalence. Unlike mortality, which is quite clear because people are either dead or alive, morbidity ranges in severity and is often problematic when measured. Some conditions are widespread in the general population such as sinusitis, arthritis, asthma, and diabetes. Potentially disabling in their impact, they are sometimes difficult to assess in their society-wide effects. As noted previously, researchers may combine mortality and morbidity into a single measure using quality- or disability-adjusted life years.

Productivity and Cost

There are important relationships between productivity and cost. Higher productivity can result in a lower unit cost, such as the average or marginal cost per unit of output if input prices remain the same. Higher productivity is commonly driven by better technology or more skilled and educated workers. Sometimes technologies are conducive to economies of scale where the cost per unit of output or average cost declines with greater levels of output, at least up to some point. In the long run, and under competitive conditions, diffusion of higher productivity technologies lowers prices as producers are forced to pass on their lower costs to consumers. Wages are impacted as higher productivity workers reap higher wages associated with their greater contribution to the value of output. Employers in competitive markets bid up the price of labor commensurate with the value of their contributions. Lower prices for consumers and higher compensation for workers explain the astonishing gains in affluence that have occurred for much of the world's population since the Industrial Revolution and the cascade of technical change that ensued. An important question is whether the Industrial Revolution will be transitory or discontinuous, as was the Neolithic Revolution. Will gains to labor productivity rise rapidly or slowly going forward? We do not know, but the health sector will surely be an important part of the story.

Production of Health

Economists, health services researchers, and others have sought to better understand the production of health—health as a product—and what factors have mattered most in that endeavor, particularly in the modern era. What were the principal causes of the transformations in modern medicine? Medicine's remarkable improvements in diagnosing and treating diseases have benefited billions of people, young and old, but studies indicate that modern medical care, so significant in explaining higher levels of health today, is not the most important reason for population-wide health, especially in lower-income and developing countries. Two more important factors are economic development and public health. Gains in per capita income correlate strongly with improvements in life expectancy and negatively with infant mortality, for example. Life expectancy is greater for those in high socioeconomic groups across different countries and within countries, although the reasons for that are not fully understood. Statistical studies have not been able to identify all factors that drive health, but we do know that economic development with all its constituent parts is very important. The distribution of economic gains is also of great importance.

One established income-related factor leading to better health is nutrition. Better nutrition improves immunological response, and studies show that better nutrition has led to greater physical height and age-appropriate weight as well as longer lives. It is particularly important in the first years of life. More recently, however, obesity has emerged as a leading public health concern in many countries, including the United States, which has some of the worst levels of obesity, especially for the lower-income strata. It has become a top public health priority.

Education is another important income-related factor tied to health. More advanced economies can better afford higher levels of education, and this correlates with better health. A knowledge of measures to prevent illness, routine family hygiene, and the ability to access information about diagnosis and treatment are all important elements in generating improved levels of health. The better educated may demand more answers from their providers and engage more fully in health-related decisions. With more information, they are better positioned to be wiser guardians of their own health.

The strong correlation between education and health does not necessarily mean an invariable direct relationship between the two. Better education does not always explain better health. An alternative theory posits that a third variable drives both education and health. This is the premium placed on the present relative to the future. Those individuals with little concern for the future are likely to put less emphasis on education and health, but those concerned about a longer time horizon will adjust their behavior to promote a relatively better future. Close attention to both education and health are important pillars of future well-being. The rate-of-time preference, near or far, is in part socially determined by the influence of parents, peers, or others. The environment of those around us impacts our own behavior. Social pressures to conform are an important part of human evolution and adopting attitudes to fit in can be seen as a survival strategy. Unfortunately, a live-for-the-moment orientation can have adverse consequences too, especially in the long run.

Although public health infrastructure is tied to economic development, many scholars, especially those in the public health community, view it as a relatively independent factor. Chapter 1 noted that even ancient civilizations recognized the importance of sanitation and cleanliness for good health, but it was not until the 19th-century development of the germ theory that modern notions of sanitation emerged. In the United States, water and sanitation systems as well as refrigeration and food safety programs were established in larger cities in the latter part of the 19th and early 20th centuries. This greatly reduced water- and food-borne disease. The timing of public health investments relative to the introduction of medicines for various diseases helps underscore the dual importance of public health. Public health measures commonly preceded medications and are responsible for much of the improvement in morbidity and mortality. From the 1920s to the 1960s, medications for diphtheria, pneumonia, scarlet fever, tuberculosis, and measles were introduced after public health measures had greatly reduced mortality. The public health infrastructure was the dominant factor in promoting better health in communities, though the advent of medications such as penicillin were major and consequential breakthroughs reducing mortality and morbidity from the middle of the 20th century.

Public health interventions include sanitation systems, access to clean water, rules for safer foods and drugs, inspections and enforcement of such rules, protection from hazardous chemicals, and occupational safety measures. They also include activities that overlap with medical care such as disease surveillance and vaccination programs. Public health measures have been found to be most effective in developing countries with high levels of infectious disease. Higher levels of economic development are associated with epidemiological transition (discussed in Chapter 3) characterized by a shift away from infectious toward degenerative disease, COVID-19 notwithstanding. But public health remains very important in identifying and mitigating risks in advanced economies where infectious disease outbreaks are expected to recur. There, multiple noninfectious risks must be managed as well. For example, the incidences of smoking and traffic safety have greatly improved with public health intervention, even as obesity and substance abuse continue to be leading noninfectious health risks.

Medical care consumes most of the resources allocated to the health sector. It is not always as effective as other drivers of health, prompting many to urge a reallocation of resources. But medical care remains important. Recent improvements in cardiovascular health and cancer, with associated gains to both years of life and quality of life, are a case in point. Figure 8.2 shows improvements in heart disease and cancer outcomes in the United States, with actual data to 2014 and estimates to 2020. Death rates for both heart disease and cancer have been in decline since the early 1990s. Change in heart disease death rates from 1969 onward is particularly noteworthy. Much of this improvement is due to medical advances.

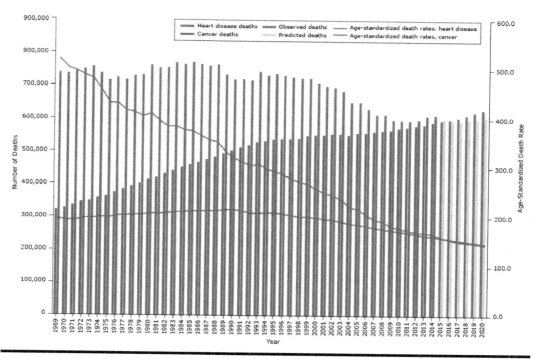

Figure 8.2   Heart Disease and Cancer Mortality in the United States 1969–2020

Source: https://www.cdc.gov/pcd/issues/2016/16_0211.htm

Heart Disease and Cancer Deaths—Trends and Projections in the United States, 1969–2020 (cdc.gov)

Individual behavior is another important variable, demonstrating the power of healthy lifestyles to make a difference. A study from the 1950s and 1960s compared lifestyles in neighboring Utah and Nevada. Utah residents had a relatively low use of alcohol, tobacco, and even caffeine, while Nevada residents were more prone to unhealthy lifestyles. Death rates were much higher in Nevada than Utah, especially for infants and middle-aged adults. Lifestyle matters, and public health measures to help manage diets, physical activity, substance abuse, and exposure to environmental risk remain of great importance.

Synopsis

Multiple factors are involved in the production of health. Scholars may differ on which factors are of greater importance, but economic growth, public health, and medical care all contribute. The long-term trend of health in the

United States has been upward with improvements in health across a variety of measures. American life expectancy at birth has increased steadily since 1860 when life expectancy was about 40. To be sure, wide-scale setbacks have retarded this trend; for example, the Civil War, the Spanish flu, and most recently the opioid epidemic and COVID-19. Figure 8.3 shows the increase in life expectancy at birth in the United States since 1960, with projections from 2015 to 2060 when life expectancy is expected to exceed 85 for the population as a whole.

Different factors have had outsized impacts on human health in different time periods. Research suggests that nutrition was a dominant factor in the mid-19th century America, yielding only to public health as a leading driver of health in the later 19th and early 20th centuries, and then to improved medical care becoming more important in the later 20th and early 21st centuries. All remain pillars of health and will drive improvements in the future.

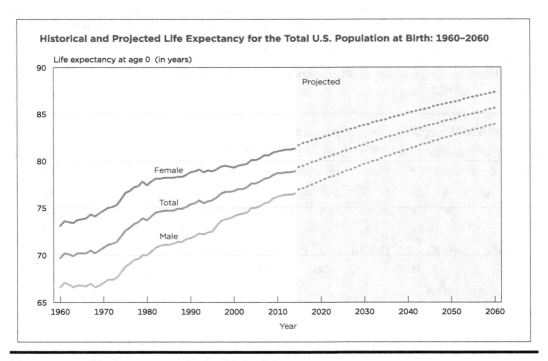

Figure 8.3   Life Expectancy in the United States

Source: www.census.gov/content/dam/Census/library/publications/2020/demo/p25-1145.pdf

Figure 8.4, published in 2018, shows that the improvement in life expectancy at birth in the United States does not compare well with other developed countries. The impact of COVID would amplify poor performance if the chart was extended to 2020 or beyond. Still, viewed together, all countries showed an improvement in life expectancy. Shaded columns represent periods of recession in the United States. Relatively poor American gains in life expectancy are not from a lack of investment in healthcare as there have been substantial health expenditures in the decades since 1960. Why then has production of life expectancy gains in the United States been wanting? Answers are multifold, but socioeconomic conditions top the list. Poverty and skewed income distribution are thought to be key factors. Also, homicide is a significant cause of death for young people, especially of color; the loss of many young men to violence skews life expectancy downward. Similarly, the opioid epidemic driven by adverse social conditions has shortened the lives of many young people. American income distribution is relatively more unequal than the comparison countries of Figure 8.4. Life expectancy is correlated with socioeconomic status and lower-income Americans have large health disparities compared to higher-income individuals. Many observers argue that these are public health issues that our system inadequately addresses. Some push the argument further and advocate for a

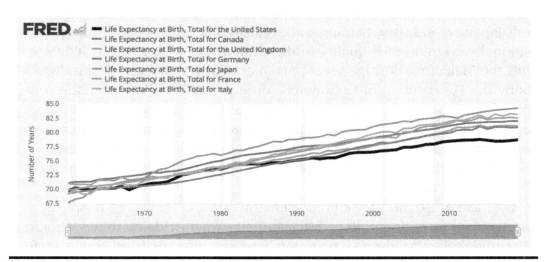

Figure 8.4　Global Comparisons of Gains in Life Expectancy

Source: https://fredblog.stlouisfed.org/2018/01/new-reflections-for-the-new-year/?
utm_source=series_page&utm_medium=related_content&utm_term=related_
resources&utm_campaign=fredblog

redistribution of wealth and income as health policy. Others believe that an expanded welfare state will only entrench existing inequality and undermine economic dynamism. It is not clear that existing poverty and institutions for social upliftment, created with the best of intentions, have been particularly effective.

Production of Health Services

Peoples' health is of paramount concern, and of secondary importance is the production of health services. The American economy was once the model of efficient production, including quality. The application of scientific management espoused by Fredrick Taylor at the beginning of the 20th century had a profound influence on the entire world. Mass production with specialized labor was put into practice by Henry Ford and other leaders in industry. Large-scale production with low average costs greatly contributed to the general rise in affluence.

Management science and operations research evolved in the mid-20th century into much of what we see today. During World War II, the success of the Navy's Operations Evaluation Group in scientifically targeting German submarines was one important application. After the war, Edward Deming advanced efficient production, especially in collaboration with Japanese industry, helping to develop statistical control techniques. National recognition for quality in the United States came in the 1980s with the Malcom Baldridge award given annually to outstanding individuals by the Department of Commerce. More recently, various management approaches and programs such as total quality management (TQM) and Lean Six Sigma production have been touted and applied to different sectors of the economy, including healthcare with the purpose of reducing waste, improving quality, and more efficiently producing and delivering goods and services.

The healthcare industry embraced many of these initiatives; hospitals, for example, were drawn to investigate better ways of doing things. Projects were undertaken to improve planning, training, inventory and supply chain management, cash management, and system-wide cooperation. But the importance of the impact is not yet clear. Clinical production decisions remain with physicians and other providers outside the realm of management discretion. The hegemony of providers impacts culture, and the culture of healthcare does not prioritize cost-saving, particularly at the expense of health. Moreover, skewed financial incentives to embrace questionable technologies and excessive resource intensity are powerful and not easily overcome. Efficiency may be embraced in healthcare settings if it does not compromise financial objectives, but all too often this is not the case. Not coincidentally, accounting systems in the health sector are not conducive to cost management. They are opaque and designed for reimbursement, not for the careful identification of cost used for management and pricing. Reform of accounting systems is a critical element for improved efficiency going forward, and while some organizations have embraced the elements of activity-based costing, an approach that better identifies cost, most have not.

One area that has made inroads with providers is the use of practice guidelines and clinical pathways, tools that help providers determine the best way forward with patients. Using such tools, researchers identify and make available the best options for physicians, nurses, and others based on studies and the broader health literature. Sometimes providers reject these tools as "cookbook medicine" and argue that they are insufficient to deal with the widespread heterogeneity of patient status that providers face. Others have been more accepting, especially integrated healthcare systems that are often able to make better use of this approach.

Production of health services has a heavy burden of regulation and compliance. Much of this burden is directed at safety and quality, at least nominally, and significantly impacts production functions. Administrative costs are higher than otherwise would be, and this is compounded by complex and costly insurance claims compliance and processing. Liability is a related concern. Malpractice insurance has both direct and indirect costs. Indirect costs are associated with defensive medicine and are thought to be much higher than direct malpractice insurance costs. Providers practice in a manner designed to reduce liability, commonly providing unnecessary care. Inappropriate care, induced by either defensive medicine or economic incentives associated with fee-for-service reimbursement is a major problem in the health sector and accounts for a large portion of high American healthcare costs.

Information Technology in Healthcare

One of the most promising areas for productivity improvement in the health sector is health information technology (HIT). For years, the health sector lagged in the use of information technology compared to finance, media, and communications owing to an absence of incentive to change. The American Recovery and Reinvestment Act of 2009 changed that. This legislation provided both carrots and sticks to encourage widespread adoption of information technology in the health sector. For example, generous subsidies were made available to hospitals, physicians, and others to develop and establish electronic scheduling, prescribing, and medical records. These capabilities, especially electronic medical records, were envisaged as a foundation that would better utilize such information. The large-scale availability of electronic data can be used with artificial intelligence to complement the efforts of providers and improve diagnosis and treatment. In other cases, artificial intelligence may be able to substitute for expensive providers and provide better, faster, and less costly health services.

Unfortunately, the implementation of HIT has not gone as well as many had hoped. Health systems and other organizations spend large sums of money establishing and operating expensive information systems with little direct compensation for their costs. Also, providers must meet market and government expectations, which includes compliance with the Health Insurance Portability and Accountability Act (HIPAA) of 1996 which has strict rules governing the protection of medical record confidentiality. With HIT, consumers enjoy more convenience, better access to their health and billing information, and improved quality. Providers can better spot medication errors, more easily identify flagged lab results, and ensure that patients comply with recommended preventive interventions. Still, widespread cost savings have yet to be realized. Health systems generally employ HIT as a complement to the services of providers, but savings are more likely to occur when HIT substitutes for providers. And that is something most providers are reluctant to welcome.

Another problem is ownership of data. Providers own information they generate and while they must provide it to each patient, they have shown reluctance to facilitate data flows between healthcare systems. Health information exchanges were meant to facilitate the easy movement of data but in practice have delivered disappointing results. Providers view data as proprietary and use it for market positioning. Actions that would make data transfer easier might also encourage consumers to substitute alternative providers. As a result, providers have used their IT systems to help lock their patient base in place. Policy that shifts ownership rights of data in favor of consumers is needed. Properly designed, it would enhance the free flow of patient data encouraging more shopping leading to lower costs and improved outcomes.

Telemedicine is an important application of HIT. Its origins are in the use of telegraph and telephone communications among providers in the 19th century and in the new technologies available by the end of the 20th century. Telemedicine using computer screens for communication is used to better link and integrate rural and remote locations. In the late 20th century, digital picture archiving and communication systems began to displace analog images, allowing radiologists to store more easily, share, and, in some cases, read images. The COVID epidemic catalyzed the use of telemedicine in 2020, as many consumers and providers rapidly switched to Zoom, WebEx, or other teleconferencing technologies. This remote format provided protection from infection but was also more convenient and efficient for many patients. In sum, the COVID epidemic served as an accelerator for the adaptation and dissemination of this technology.

Conclusion

Healthcare IT is only in its infancy. We can expect more advanced utilization of information technology to help providers determine optimal clinical pathways. For example, research has found a pervasive lack of compliance with clinical guidelines for many conditions such as substance abuse, diabetes, and cardiovascular conditions. Greater use of HIT can help by reducing the variations observed in the treatment of such common conditions. We know that the use of the best technologies and appropriate inputs improves production. But also of great importance governing decision-making, and underrecognized by many, is the role of culture. As noted, the culture of healthcare is not primarily focused on efficiency. Social and economic institutions such as hospitals are inordinately structured to serve the interests of providers rather than patients and consumers, or society more generally. Moreover, the ethic of providers is not to optimize health weighing costs and benefits but to maximize it, though ironically the United States does neither. A cultural change among providers would require an important ethical recalibration. Schools of medicine and health sciences can start by educating providers to better understand efficiency and the ethics of opportunity cost. The COVID epidemic pitted providers and the public health community against the business community, among others, in how best to manage the tradeoff between lives and livelihoods. As noted previously, the health community has been reluctant to recognize the full cost of its pandemic response, whether monetary, such as lost output, or negative impact on satisfaction, such as the discomfort of mask wearing that many perceive to be a serious issue. The health community commonly downplays such trad-eoffs and characterizes putting a price on life to benchmark and limit costs such as lockdowns as unethical. It is not, and the sooner this is recognized, the sooner we will advance to greater levels of efficiency in healthcare and social welfare more generally.

Chapter 9

Healthcare and Macroeconomics: Productivity, the Economy, and Monetary Policy

Introduction

Chapter 8 explored the concept of productivity, emphasizing the relationships between input, technology, and output. Chapter 9 discusses the outlook for productivity, growth, and the macroeconomy with an emphasis on the health sector. As noted, economists vary in their outlook on future productivity and the ability of technology to catalyze rapid improvement in per capita income. Pessimists emphasize a weak productivity outlook associated with available technologies as well as those expected in the foreseeable future. The rapidly growing low-productivity health sector underscores how productivity growth may flail; some studies even show negative productivity in healthcare. Sluggish productivity in the health sector, given its size, adversely impacts the overall standard of living in the United States.

Optimists, on the other hand, see brighter days ahead. They see rapid gains in our standard of living, including health, driven by a host of technologies, both known and yet to come. They see an increasingly educated American and global society with sufficient dynamic and entrepreneurial drive to successfully invent, innovate, and cultivate higher levels of prosperity everywhere. Although malaise and despair have marked the

DOI: 10.4324/9781003186137-12

American outlook in the past, optimists caution about counting America out. Pessimism has not been a winning bet.

The first of the three primary sections in this chapter, the introductory part, describes the Gordon thesis with an emphasis on the growth of productivity. In 2016, Robert Gordon of Northwestern University published *The Rise and Fall of American Growth*, which claims that the best days of the United States are behind it with respect to the rate of improvement in the standard of living. His thesis generated considerable controversy about the trajectory of US productivity growth. Emerging technologies, institutional reform, and productivity potential in health are key elements in this story given the size of the American health sector. Promising use of newer technologies, it argues, will not be sufficient to substantially boost productivity and efficiency. New technologies include mobile communications and associated applications, robotics, and electronic medical records paired with artificial intelligence. Institutional change will occur too, but Gordon does not see productivity gains of the magnitude enjoyed by previous generations. It is argued here that this view may be too pessimistic, particularly if the health sector is transformed toward much higher productivity gains.

The second section describes differential rates of price appreciation in the health sector compared to economy-wide inflation. It explores the impact of more muted medical "inflation" on economy-wide inflation and monetary policy, noting that a successful inflation policy must increasingly take account of the health sector. The health sector, now about 20% of the economy, has been a haven of rapid price appreciation. Data show the disparity between sectoral "inflation" and economy-wide price growth. Health sector prices have risen more rapidly than most other sectors and they have been a crutch complementing easy monetary policies as the United States sought a 2% inflation rate. Easy monetary policy includes setting low interest rates and providing ample liquidity in the economy to encourage spending and investment. Monetary authorities in other developed countries have not faced rapidly rising health prices, at least to the extent experienced in the United States, and this has undermined the success of their monetary policy efforts to resist deflation. When monetary policy pivots to fighting inflation, sustained high health sector price growth will aggravate the inflationary pressures of expansionary monetary and fiscal policies.

The third section explores how the health sector has affected the inequality of wealth and income in the United States. Inequality is a widespread concern affecting both economic growth and differing conceptions of equity. This section examines data showing that the top 1% of income distribution increasingly consists of those from the health sector. Advancement of greater numbers and proportions of health-sector workers into the ranks of America's elite is a function of both growth of healthcare and high levels of compensation for many occupations.

US Productivity and the Health Sector

Many economists hold that the US economy has a long-run annual growth potential of approximately 2%, or perhaps a bit higher. This is driven by productivity growth of a little more than 1% and labor force growth of somewhat under 1%. The productivity growth of 1% is substantially less than the United States enjoyed in previous decades. Economists often group periods of time by waves of new technology. Walt Rostow, an economic historian and well-known for his influential *Stages of Growth* in the 1950s and 1960s, saw long cycles driven by new technology, the relative prices of raw materials and finished goods, and a host of other factors. He called these Kondratieff cycles, after a Soviet economist credited with pioneering long-cycle work. Rostow identified five such long cycles from the late 18th to late 20th centuries. He was generally an optimist and believed technology would lead to sustained high and higher standards of living globally. This chapter and the subsequent one concur with that view and assert that the health sector will serve as a leader in moving economic development forward.

In contrast, Gordon in *The Rise and Fall of American Growth* takes a pessimistic view. He shows how new technologies became widespread after the Civil War and fueled a century of transformative change. A key factor was urbanization and linkages to clean water, sanitation, heating, electric power, appliances, and telephone systems. The advent of air conditioning was also of importance as it created more productive environments at home and at work than the humble electric fan could provide. Rural areas eventually caught up to the cities and made available most of these amenities. Such advances brought dramatic improvement to America's standard of living including extended life expectancy as well as reduced infant and childhood mortality.

Gordon's work employs a paradigm consisting of three industrial revolutions driven primarily by clusters of technology. The first, beginning in the late 18th century, was led by steam power, cotton, and textile manufacture. The second began after the Civil War and was fueled by steel, electricity, elevators, chemicals and plastics, appliances, internal combustion engines, and air transport. Additional innovations at this critical stage included telephones, movies, radio, and television. This wave of technology had played out by the mid to late 20th century. It was followed by another wave that included computers, the internet, cell phones, bar codes, ATMs, and a shift to large, comprehensive retailers such as Walmart and Amazon. This latest wave, however, has not had the same impact on productivity or the standard of living as previous ones. Growth rates have fallen with a conspicuous erosion in the improvement of the standard of living for the younger generations.

This second industrial revolution employed electric power and the internal combustion engine combined with large-scale production and other technologies to yield prolonged high rates of productivity gain in manufacturing and agriculture. Gordon asserts that improved technologies since the late 20th century have had less impact on productivity. The reason for this can be seen in information technologies and robotics. They certainly helped and contributed to economic development, but despite giving a transitory boost to productivity starting in the mid-1990s, their impact has not been of the same order of magnitude as previous generations of new technology. Gordon does not believe that these or other new technologies will be as consequential for future growth in the United States as were those integrated into the fabric of the economy in the late 19th to mid-20th centuries. For example, he shows that the output per hour increased by an average of 2.82% from 1920 to 1970. Hours worked per person declined in this time interval and hence output per person was somewhat less, growing at 2.41%. The net effect substantially boosted the standard of living as measured by disposable income, or income after taxes. Inflation-adjusted median per capita disposable income increased annually by 2.25% from 1920 to 1970. Gordon sees this slowing to 0.30% from 2015 to 2040. Much of this change can be explained by an underwhelming impact from new technology but also by other factors such as demographic and fiscal headwinds. Future productivity growth is put at 1.2% annually, about 1.1% lower than the output per hour from 1920 to 2014. Much of this is then offset by an aging and retiring population, inequality, and fiscal retrenchment, putting median per capita disposable income growth much lower at 0.30%.

As it turned out, there has been improvement in recent years, as shown in Figure 9.1 which depict annual productivity gains from 1950 to 2020. Since 2011, labor productivity increased which may be explained by tax cuts, deregulation, and the sharp COVID-induced economic downturn. Recessions commonly boost productivity if employment falls faster than output, a\ development observed in the Great Recession in 2009. These occurrences

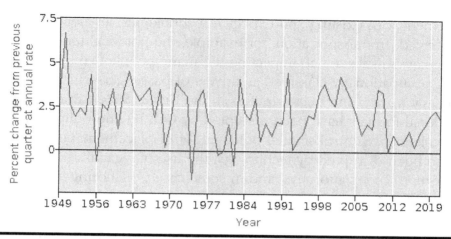

Figure 9.1   US Labor Productivity (change in output per hour in nonfarm business)
Source: https://www.bls.gov/lpc/

are arguably of a temporary nature, at least from a demand perspective. Investment is more important for productivity in the long run and since the COVID-induced recession of 2020, investment levels have recovered and may increase further, which bodes well for productivity.

Recessions, for all the pain they bring, are times of general economic renewal; suppliers are forced to cut back and often let their least-productive workers and equipment go. The ratio of capital to labor increases, and with it, labor productivity. Employers are forced to respond to changing conditions. The COVID-induced recession ushered in a new era of work from home, telemedicine, and accelerated shifts to online shopping, among other changes. Such developments promise greater sustained productivity. Periods of rapid economic growth also spur innovation and productivity. A strong economy can lead to shortages of labor, and this in turn induces employers to become more efficient—for example, in their use of more and better capital equipment.

Services now account for the lion's share of the value added in the US economy, put at 77% in 2019 by the World Bank. Obviously, the future of American productivity growth rests on higher service productivity. Services have been inherently labor intensive, making it more difficult to employ productivity-enhancing technology than is the case in manufacturing or agriculture. A pessimistic assessment is that not much will change here as technology cannot easily substitute for the services of teachers, barbers, healthcare providers, and others who rely on face-to-face contact with customers. In contrast, an optimistic perspective sees considerable room for improvement with existing and expected technologies, let alone those not yet conceived. In transportation, for example, the potential for self-driving vehicles may be substantial, impacting the many people (4.6 million in 2019) who are occupationally classified as drivers of passenger vehicles, delivery vans, heavy trucks, and tractor-trailers in the United States. In education, conventional formats have been disrupted by COVID and online options have accelerated with substantial potential for displacement. Legal services have also been disrupted by technology, the use of legal assistants as substitutes for more costly attorneys, and in some cases, offshoring.

The health sector is one of the most important elements of the service sector with potential for economy-wide benefits if improved productivity can be found. With over 20 million workers in healthcare and social assistance alone, its impact on cost-saving could be considerable. *The Rise and Fall of American Growth* pays much attention to improvement in health achieved in the span of years from 1870 to 1970. It explains how primary factors for improved health were better nutrition and better public health. Medical care was of less importance. But the case can be made that Gordon's view does not sufficiently recognize the increased importance of medical care to health in more developed stages of growth. He also does not adequately explore the production of health services and the potential for new technology, deregulation, improved management, and better institutions to lift productivity in the health sector and more broadly in the economy. This shortcoming alone poses a challenge to his view of anemic growth in the coming decades.

High rates of cost increase in the health sector surely will not be sustained indefinitely. Further outsized growth of health spending will impact nonhealth compensation and the standard of living. Eventually, the nonhealth standard of living will decline as healthcare expands rapidly, especially in an environment of low productivity. The shift of compensation from wages to health benefits is part of the reason workers commonly believe their incomes have stagnated. A declining nonhealth standard of living is likely to be met with a political backlash and accelerated reform of healthcare institutions. Ironically, increases in health spending at the expense of the nonhealth standard of living could undermine life expectancy and other measures of health and well-being given the strong correlation between per capita income and health.

Institutional change has been evolving and can be expected to curb the growth of health expenditures. Expanded use of consumer-driven healthcare with high deductibles has eased the problem of excessive insurance and slowed cost growth. Consumers now have more incentive to shop and conserve. A growing bipartisan chorus from the policy community is calling for reform of occupational licensure and other barriers to entry in the health professions, which has the potential to improve the efficiency of production. Perhaps of greatest potential impact at this time is the prospect of greater use of monopsony power held by government. Recall that monopsony power refers to market power held by buyers. Such power can force sellers to their minimum price before they withdraw from the market. The expansion of Medicaid and the aging of the population into Medicare have boosted the bargaining power of government, a key purchaser of health services. Lowering Medicare eligibility to, say, 60 from the current 65 would increase that power even more.

A single or all-payer system would be most significant for accruing monopsony power in the purchase of health services. An all-payer system features multiple payers, possibly including private ones, but coordinates payment rates for all; for example, Maryland has successfully employed an all-payer system for hospital payment since 1977. However, acquiring monopsony power is not the same as exercising it. The history of regulation suggests that policy is often captured and shaped by the regulated at the expense of the consuming public. The suppliers and vested interests routinely appear at regulatory hearings and lobby to make their case much more often than the public. Consequently, regulated rates are often high— higher than would occur in competitive markets—and it is also possible that rates paid to providers in a single-payer system would be advantageous to providers as well given the lobbying clout of the healthcare industry. In any case, the likelihood of a rapid and complete shift to such healthcare finance is not high given industry and ideological resistance. More gradual payment reform leading to more price-sensitive demand along with an associated evolution of productivity-enhancing technology is more probable. More price-sensitive demand incentivizes producers and providers to reduce costs as a market strategy. But payments that are too low will cause suppliers to withdraw, as we see in the market for Medicaid services, where many providers have been reluctant to participate.

A shift toward national health insurance in the United States, however pronounced, will change incentives from cost-increasing to cost-decreasing. Providers will face more price-sensitive demand and shift toward becoming price takers rather than price makers. Under this format, they will find it more difficult to raise prices and employ costly technologies. A single payer has greater power to impose prices than a fragmented health insurance industry where insurers can pass off costs to employers. Cost-reducing technologies will become relatively more attractive, and some shifting away from cost-increasing technology can be expected.

The health sector has multiple paths to bend the cost curve down. For example, a range of new technologies including artificial intelligence, mobile communications, new and improved biometric sensors, 3-D printing, and robotics promise market disruption and costs savings. A platform for such advances has already been largely established with the widespread use of electronic medical records, and while savings from healthcare IT have been thus far underwhelming, this may not continue especially if technology increasingly becomes a substitute for high-cost providers rather than merely a complement to their services.

The differential between GDP and health expenditure growth has slowed in recent decades, and it could conceivably reverse in a sustained manner to the point where GDP growth exceeds that of health expenditures. After the Great Recession, there was a significant slowdown in health expenditure growth. Many economists attribute consumer-driven healthcare for this change, but other factors such as the growth of low priced Medicaid and drug patent expirations were important too. There were four years in the decade from 2010 to 2020 when GDP growth exceeded that of national health expenditures. There is no reason to assume such an event cannot happen again on a sustained basis.

Healthcare Inflation, and Monetary Policy

The late Uwe Reinhardt of Princeton University consistently emphasized healthcare prices as the reason for high health expenditures. For example, Americans pay more for branded prescription drugs and many medical procedures than other developed nations. Americans are not outliers in the utilization of health services. Hospital use and physician visits are similar, and in some cases lower, than in other developed nations. But prices are high and generally rising, and this leads to high health expenditures by global standards. Rising prices are also a concern for monetary policy.

That policy is largely overseen by the Federal Reserve Bank (Fed), which has been targeting inflation. The Fed targeted an inflation rate of 2% but eased that in 2020 to an average of 2% over the business cycle. The average rate of consumer inflation measured by the consumer price index (CPI) from 2012 to 2019 was about 1.5%, somewhat less than the target. There was then even some deflation from February to April or May in 2020, in response to the economic collapse due to the COVID epidemic. The Fed was not alone in struggling to support its target; other developed nations did worse. One of the advantages the Fed enjoys in combating deflationary pressures is the American healthcare sector, particularly prices paid by private insurers. In this respect, rapidly rising healthcare prices were positive for the economy. Figures 9.2 and 9.3 show how health sector prices led and buoyed the GDP deflator from 2008 to 2018 and how prices paid by the private sector have led health price growth. Note the much lower rate of price increases for Medicare and Medicaid, the two largest public sector insurance programs, depicted in Figure 9.3, which shows hospital inpatient prices. Hospital outpatient price increases are similarly led by private payers.

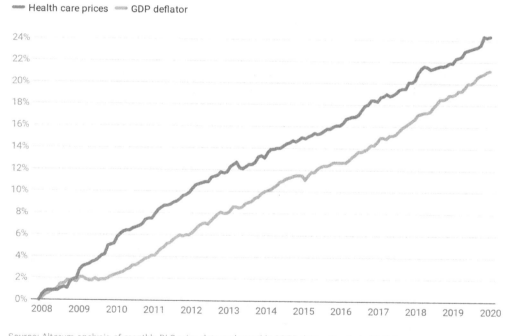

Cumulative percent change since December 2007 in health care prices and GDP deflator

Source: Altarum analysis of monthly BLS price data and monthly GDPD data. · Created with Datawrapper

Figure 9.2   Healthcare Price Increases Lead to Inflation

Source: www.healthsystemtracker.org/indicator/spending/price-index/

Prices & Use Indices, 2020

Accessed September 17, 2021.

Reprinted with permission of the Peterson-Kaiser Health System Tracker.

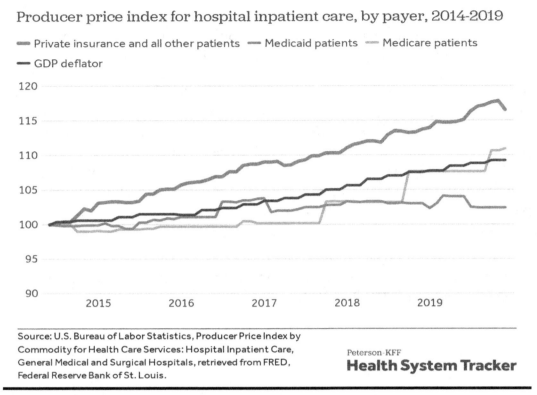

Producer price index for hospital inpatient care, by payer, 2014-2019

■ Private insurance and all other patients ■ Medicaid patients ■ Medicare patients
■ GDP deflator

Source: U.S. Bureau of Labor Statistics, Producer Price Index by Commodity for Health Care Services: Hospital Inpatient Care, General Medical and Surgical Hospitals, retrieved from FRED, Federal Reserve Bank of St. Louis.

Peterson-KFF
Health System Tracker

Figure 9.3   Private Payors Lead Public Payors in Inpatient Price Increases

Source: www.healthsystemtracker.org/indicator/spending/price-index/

Prices & Use Indices, 2020

Accessed September 17, 2021.

Reprinted with permission of the Peterson-Kaiser Health System Tracker.

The impact of the health sector on inflation is underappreciated. Medical care is a relatively smaller share of the CPI than it is of consumption, a fact explained by the high contribution of health insurance, which is excluded from measures of household spending. Only out-of-pocket spending is included. Figure 9.4, which breaks down the Department of Labor's CPI, and Figure 9.5, which shows the Department of Commerce's larger role of health in personal consumption, underscore the difference. Medical care accounted for about 9% of the CPI in 2021, but health spending accounted for 17% of personal consumption in 2019 and then fell back to 16% in the second quarter of 2021 during the COVID epidemic. The consumption of goods rose during this period. Arguably, the CPI is a misleading measure, at least with respect to health expenditures.

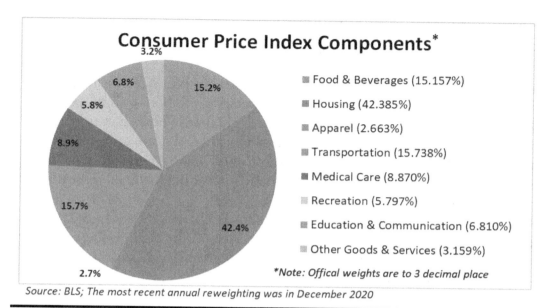

Figure 9.4   Breakdown of Consumer Price Index

Source: https://www.advisorperspectives.com/dshort/updates/2021/09/14/
components-of-the-cpi-august-2021

Reprinted with permission of Advisor Perspectives.

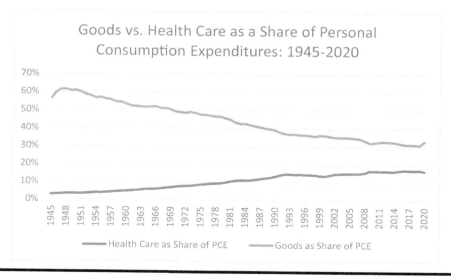

Figure 9.5   Increasing Importance of Healthcare in US Consumption

Source: https://apps.bea.gov/iTable/iTable.cfm?reqid=19&step=2#reqid=19&step=2&
isuri=1&1921=survey

The impact of medical and other healthcare inflationary pressures on economy-wide inflation is an important influence to consider. Healthcare has been a support for the Fed when deflationary concern prevailed. Should that crutch be removed in a sluggish economy, the consequences for monetary policy could be substantial. American monetary conditions would more closely resemble those in parts of Europe and Japan where interest rates have been even lower, and in some cases, negative. Negative interest rates are problematic and this prospect for the United States is generally not welcomed. Among other things, negative interest rates blunt the effectiveness of traditional monetary policy.

Alternatively, as monetary policy shifts to combating inflation, the health sector will remain pivotal. Expansionary monetary and fiscal policies to boost output and employment can lead to inflationary pressures in a supply constrained environment, which will become endemic if a wage–price spiral is established. Inflationary expectations have much to do with this as both workers and employers plan for inflation in wage demands and pricing strategy. Such a situation existed in the 1970s and the cycle was only broken by very tight monetary policy accompanied by a painful recession in the early 1980s. Some economists fear a replay. Rising healthcare prices at rates greater than economy-wide price increases would render containment of inflation more difficult. High levels of inflation are detrimental to economic growth for several reasons, including a rising uncertainty that can undermine investment. Inflation has distributional effects too. For example, inflation erodes the real value of debt, which can be advantageous for borrowers with fixed low interest rates. In general, borrowers benefit from inflation at the expense of lenders, and many borrowers are from the lower-income strata.

Equity and the Health Sector

It is difficult to understand the current political and social tensions in the United States without addressing equity. Wealth and income distributions are relatively skewed in the United States compared to other developed countries, and the spread has widened. Many Marxists believe the contradictions in our society and institutions such as social production where public dollars in direct subsidies, tax incentives, and public education, for example, support the profit-making activities of private enterprises and private appropriation where profits are captured entirely by private investors, combined with gaping inequity will lead to a breakdown of the social order. One interpretation is that taxation and levels of debt necessary to support education, health, and an expansive range of social support will become unbearable and precipitate a transformative fiscal crisis to restore broad-based legitimacy. However, capitalism has not yet collapsed, and if China is an indicator, Marxists and Leninists who emphasize the primacy of the Communist Party have gravitated to state capitalism. As the past 30 years have shown, there is little appetite in the world for state appropriation of all private property and Soviet-style central planning. But surely the United States faces fiscal as well as demographic, educational, and health-sector headwinds that will blunt growth and add stress to social stability. One does not have to be a Marxist to be concerned about inequity and its destabilizing influence. The role of income and wealth distribution in promoting the greater good is vital to the social fabric of the United States.

As noted, wealth has become very concentrated in the United States. In 1963, the 90th percentile of Americans ranked by their accumulated personal wealth had 5.82 times the wealth of the 50th percentile and the 99th percentile had a multiple of 35.52. By 2016, these respective disparities had widened to multiples of 12.19 and 106.86. In the first quarter of 2021, the top 1% owned 32% of the net worth in the country, while the 90th to 99th percentile possessed 38%, the 50–90th percentile had 28%, leaving a paltry 2% of net worth for the bottom 50%. Transfer payments and progressive taxation have provided some amelioration of this gaping inequity, but a sense of frustration is palpable and has arguably fueled the support for disruptive politics on both the right and left.

Figure 9.6 shows income shares measured in percentage in 2018, comparing different quintiles; it contrasts income distribution with and without income taxes and transfers. Transfers are primarily designed to assist low-income persons and households. As can be seen, income taxes and transfers markedly reduce disparities, but the top 20% enjoyed a very large allocation, however measured, even with a much higher tax burden. The average income of the highest income quintile after taxes and transfers was $243,900 compared to $37,700 for the lowest quintile.

The role of the health sector in increasing the wealth and income disparities is not well understood. A persistent outpacing of health sector growth

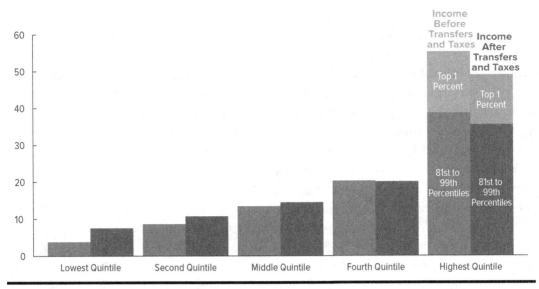

Figure 9.6   Income Distribution

Source: https://www.cbo.gov/publication/55413

relative to GDP growth has impacted the sociology of who is in the top percentiles of American income distribution. Greater levels of health-sector employment drive this as does formidable occupational earnings, especially for those with high levels of education.

Occupational licensure, ostensibly to protect the public from shoddy quality, is part of the explanation for this income distribution, as described in Chapter 5, but other elements of market power are important too. High levels of schooling, lengthy learning requirements, and limited opportunities for medical education constitute a familiar barrier, but other health-related occupations have followed suit with more rigorous education and licensure. Over time, educational standards have risen. Now pharmacists in the United States must earn a doctorate in order to practice. Physical therapy has also shifted to doctoral standards. The two- or three-year nursing programs offered at American community colleges are under threat from the four-year university programs. This raising of the occupational bar has further increased costs and reduced the relative supply of healthcare personnel. Limitations in supply when combined with a relatively unconstrained consumer demand liberally fueled by third-party fee-for-service payment have had the predictable consequence of driving up the incomes of providers and others employed in the health sector.

Figure 9.7 plots the change in excess pay (pay greater than opportunity cost) in the hospital, financial, and legal sectors along with eating and drinking establishments. Payments greater than that necessary to attract and retain workers are considered rents by economists and are not necessary for the efficient allocation of resources. Economic rents are like profits in that they are revenue greater than cost; however, profits serve the economic purpose of attracting supply, whereas economic rents have no such impact. In practice, matters are not so simple and economists refer to the term quasi-rents. Quasi-rents apply when there is heterogeneity in the marketplace. So, for example, not all investment bankers or physicians are of equal quality. While excessive pay does not increase the total supply of bankers and physicians, it does lead to higher average quality as employers recruit top-flight talent. Monopoly or market power is a major reason rents, or excess payments, exist for prolonged periods. Figure 9.8 shows that "excess pay" grew fastest in the hospital sector relative to securities and investments, banking, and legal services. In contrast, eating and drinking establishments were

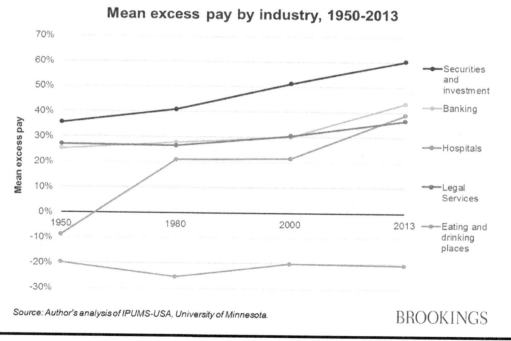

Mean excess pay by industry, 1950-2013

Source: Author's analysis of IPUMS-USA, University of Minnesota.

BROOKINGS

Figure 9.7 Economic Rents in the United States

Source: www.brookings.edu/research/make-elites-compete-why-the-1-earn-so-much-and-what-to-do-about-it/

Reprinted with permission of the Brookings Institution.

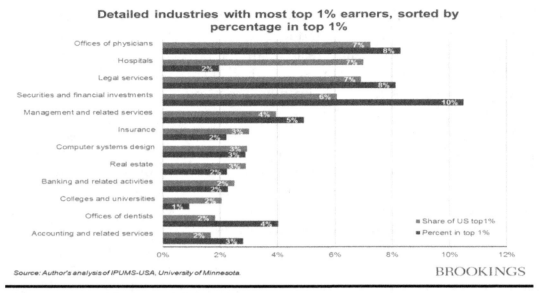

Detailed industries with most top 1% earners, sorted by percentage in top 1%

Source: Author's analysis of IPUMS-USA, University of Minnesota.   BROOKINGS

Figure 9.8   Healthcare and the Top 1%

Source: www.brookings.edu/research/make-elites-compete-why-the-1-earn-so-much-and-what-to-do-about-it/

Reprinted with permission of the Brookings Institution.

found to have inadequate compensation, which helps explain the high turnover in that sector.

Figure 9.8 provides a profile of the top 1% of earners in the United States for 2013. Elements of legal services and the financial sector, including banking and accounting services, inhabit this niche. Physicians and hospital workers are also at the top of the list whether measured by most top 1% earners or percentage in the top 1%. In view of this outsized earning profile, one understands why reducing barriers to entry has become an increasingly attractive option to policy analysts. Lowered barriers can mean greater access to the healthcare professions, and by means of that opening, the competitiveness of the health sector can be improved and price pressures that compound economic rents can be contained.

Conclusion

Many Americans know by direct experience that the health sector costs too much. Hospital charges are often astronomical and the source of significant personal bankruptcies. Moreover, there is a steady drumbeat of outrage in the media about price gouging, especially for new but also older drugs. Even so, the health sector remains an oasis of privilege, protected from domestic and international price competition. It provides ready employment opportunities and is seen by students as a safe career path; they flock to health occupations in large part because they know that it is where the money and jobs are. Health and pre-health degrees are very popular and have become essential for the financial viability of many universities. At the national level, the Department of Education reports that about 19% of bachelor's degrees were in the biological or biomedical sciences and the health professions for the 2018–19 academic year. These fields accounted for about 18% of master's degrees and an astounding 48% of doctoral degrees. Some economists have pointed to the opportunity cost of allocating so many of our talented students to the health sector at the expense of other important fields such as engineering or the arts.

Improvements to efficiency in healthcare are needed. Along with improved awareness of what is not worth paying for, urgent attention should be directed at how to better produce health and health services. Of course, the impact on the macroeconomy of the United States has a significant bearing, especially in the long run, affecting our standard of living as well as our health. Given its expansive reach, growth policy in the United States should focus more on the health sector to boost GDP, strengthen our social fabric, and help ensure that America maintains its global leadership. The stakes are high.

Chapter 10

Healthcare Institutions, Technology, Ethics, and the Path Forward

Introduction

Previous chapters explored the evolution of the health sector and the roles of institutions that continue to shape its performance. They discussed the problems of asymmetric information, market power that relies in part on occupational control, the role of insurance, and allocative efficiency. They included some historical perspectives to provide a context for those problems. And they underscored the importance of productivity-driven technology in healthcare and the wider economy. An American health sector that relied on the foundations of ancient learning at the time of the nation's founding has in 200 years become a world-class leader in medical and health sciences. In the last century, the health sector expanded rapidly, outpacing the fast-growing economy and quintupling its share of GDP. Scientific knowledge and technology led to improvement in public health and medical care and together they doubled life expectancy, greatly reduced infant and child mortality, and opened new vistas for curative medicine.

Even so, the health sector today is a mixed blessing. It provides well-paid employment in many occupations and is largely protected from international and domestic competition. Its output of restored or improved health is unambiguously good and promotes both individual and social well-being. But productivity in the health sector lags and it has displaced other sectors

DOI: 10.4324/9781003186137-13

of the economy with higher productivity. Wages for the middle class have stagnated because dwindling productivity gains partly support health benefits instead of pushing up pay. Because of this, the middle class, a pillar of social stability, is threatened; the health sector is in part responsible. So, what is to be done?

At the outset, this book sought to establish the importance of institutions and technology, arguing that they can, and should, evolve to usher in a transformative era of productivity change. This can yield, if not lower costs, much more restrained cost growth and more cost-effective care. Higher health-sector productivity can improve economy-wide growth and boost real earnings. The status quo has worked well for providers up to now, but the sector is ripe for both market and nonmarket disruption.

Overview of Health Systems

The term system implies a level of coordination and integration that some observers believe does not accord with the American health sector. This sector, after all, is institutionally complex with a multitude of players. Certainly, there are organizational systems within American healthcare such as HMOs and military healthcare that are well-coordinated in terms of finance and the delivery of a wide range of services. But much of the health sector is not so well integrated. In some respects, health is like other parts of the economy that are not seen as systems such as manufacturing or agriculture. Nevertheless, there is a widespread perception of American healthcare as a system consisting of the totality of resources, organizations, and institutions oriented to the production of health. Resources are inputs in this model and a primary input is human capital. Healthcare is labor intensive once the start-up requirements of land, capital, and infrastructure for buildings have been met but the sector is becoming more capital intensive as expensive equipment and information technology evolve. In this enterprise, entrepreneurship and technology have become inputs in the production process and both are of great importance along with organizational leadership and governance. Economic, social, and cultural institutions shape the performance and conduct of the health sector as participants necessarily conform to laws, rules, and norms. The qualities of all these variables, from workforce to institutions, are critical factors of performance in the production of health services.

The success of a healthcare system can be measured by health outcomes, cost, and access. Health service researchers often emphasize quality as well;

however, economists are not always in agreement about how much quality is desirable. Optimal quality, balancing costs and benefits, conforms to efficiency criteria whereas maximizing quality does not. Over the long run, innovation and dynamism are important, which can be seen both in the development of new technologies and improvements in management and organization. Another long-run concern is sustainability. Health spending growth exceeding GDP growth is not sustainable indefinitely, but it may be efficient in the short-run, or even intermediate-run, if costs are justified by outsized benefits relative to other opportunities in the economy.

Our conception of "healthcare systems" at the present time is evolving. There is increasing recognition of the social determinants of health. We have seen the importance of public health measures in increasing life expectancy just as we have seen how socioeconomic status is a leading driver of health. But until recently, social services and social conditions were not regarded as a responsibility of the health sector. This is changing and some countries and communities are now integrating social services and healthcare to great effect. For example, homelessness in every community is associated with poor health, but mitigation is possible by a simple means: The placement of the homeless in sound accommodation has been found to reduce hospital admissions and an array of other health services. Averted medical costs borne by the public sector can be substantial and help justify the expense of housing for the homeless. Social service intervention in cases of substance abuse or problematic living conditions for the aged can similarly have a large impact on health and healthcare costs.

Finance of the health sector is of particular importance in driving performance; financing impacts incentives and incentives affect performance. Fee-for-service payment relying largely on third-party payers—which historically dominated American healthcare reimbursement—is a recipe for excessive care, both quantitatively and qualitatively. Consumers want the best healthcare and without budget constraints; few seek bargains; everyone wants premium services. Providers and suppliers respond by meeting consumer demand and handsomely enriching themselves. Capitated payment of fixed monthly or annual amounts to integrated organizations supplying both finance and care is an alternative with a long history in the United States, but it has generally been fiercely resisted by providers. The reason is that capitated payment of a fixed amount per month or year shifts incentives for providers; placing them at risk. Studies on the quality of care in different settings are mixed in their assessments but suggest that quality of care for chronic conditions may sometimes be compromised in capitated settings. Another alternative to fee-for-service care is the use of salaries, perhaps with performance-related bonuses or withholds. This is increasingly common in large organizations that have come to dominate much of healthcare. Salaried providers, even with incentives, tend to have less financial cause to over or underutilize care. As with any salaried worker, however, the issues of shirking and reduced productivity are ever present. All three—fee-for-service, capitation, and salaries—are used by private as well as public health insurance programs.

Public payers have greater monopsony power than private payers and can often compel lower payment rates. Certainly, in the United States, commercial and all private insurers tend to pay more than Medicaid and Medicare. The UK established a national health service (NHS) NHS after the Second World War that provides and pays for much of the care for their population. Thanks to it, the UK has achieved first-world levels of population health at much lower cost per person than the United States. Most other developed nations have been reluctant to go so far down the road of nationalizing the health sector. In most developed countries, the provision of care remains private, but healthcare finance relies more on public insurance than in the United States. Canada, for example, has a national health insurance program called Medicare that covers hospitalization, physician services, and some other forms of care. It is administered by the provinces and jointly financed by the provinces and the federal government.

Germany relies on not-for-profit and occupationally aligned sickness funds for most healthcare payments; their people have a choice in selecting their sickness funds. The German model, which pairs health insurance with employment, was something of a template for the Clinton healthcare reform effort. Switzerland has compulsory health insurance that can be supplemented with private insurance; dozens of not-for-profit insurers in Switzerland provide a range of options. Figure 10.1 shows health spending per capita using purchasing parity dollars that adjust exchange rates to reflect purchasing power. The United States is clearly the costliest, and the large and well-financed private sector explains much of this. In contrast, other developed countries rely more heavily on direct or indirect government finance of health services, and private insurance is more limited, often as a supplement to public entitlements. Germany has a means test to determine the eligibility to opt out of the national system of sickness funds and use private insurance as an alternative.

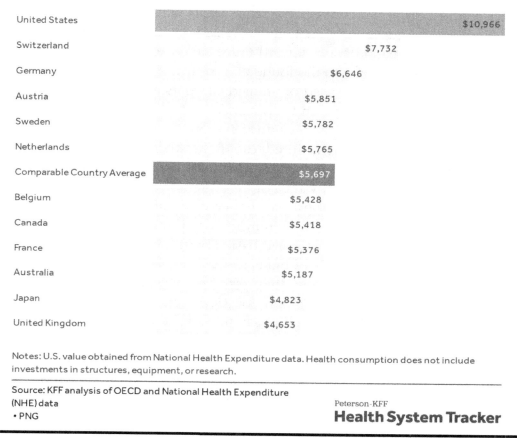

Health consumption expenditures per capita, U.S. dollars, PPP adjusted, 2019

United States	$10,966
Switzerland	$7,732
Germany	$6,646
Austria	$5,851
Sweden	$5,782
Netherlands	$5,765
Comparable Country Average	$5,697
Belgium	$5,428
Canada	$5,418
France	$5,376
Australia	$5,187
Japan	$4,823
United Kingdom	$4,653

Notes: U.S. value obtained from National Health Expenditure data. Health consumption does not include investments in structures, equipment, or research.

Source: KFF analysis of OECD and National Health Expenditure (NHE) data
• PNG

Peterson-KFF
Health System Tracker

Figure 10.1   Health Expenditures per Capita for Selected OECD Member States (2019)

Source: www.healthsystemtracker.org/chart-collection/health-spending-u-s-compare-countries/#item-start

How does health spending in the US compare to other countries?

By Rabah Kamal, Giorlando Ramirez, and Cynthia Cox of the Kaiser Family Foundation.

Accessed September 17, 2021.

Reprinted with permission of the Peterson-Kaiser Health System Tracker.

Ethics and Ideology

Ethical dimensions to healthcare issues in the United States are not sufficiently addressed in philosophical terms, at least with the use of more formal foundations of philosophical thought even with the abundance of highly educated people in the field, including those holding at least a nominal Doctor of Philosophy (Ph.D.). More engagement with philosophy and ethics would help as we consider the large issues pertaining to healthcare. For example, the question of entitlement rights is central and of growing importance as the nation edges toward universal coverage. In considering such rights, we might refer to the foundation principles of the American Revolution, which was premised on individual rights and a range of freedoms protected from invasive and capricious government restraint. Over time, and particularly in the 20th century, the public sector evolved to provide an array of entitlements in education, healthcare, and other forms of social welfare. Adherents of classical liberalism see that welfare as an encroachment on the original values of the American Revolution premised by John Locke's conception of private property and liberty. They worry about the erosion of incentives and individual responsibility. Social justice to them is the equal right to extensive basic liberties consistent with similar liberties for others. It is not about rights to publicly provided goods and services. What economic entitlement, they ask, did Benjamin Franklin, George Washington, or Thomas Jefferson fight for? One wonders how they would view the welfare state. Is it enough to say times have changed or has the revolution been betrayed?

Perhaps, Rousseau's notion of the social contract, advanced in the 18th century, accords with a more interventionist state in providing freedom from hardship, even at the expense of individual liberty and private property. Today's US economy is vastly more prosperous and complex than Rousseau's. Inequality and questions of social justice are matters of widespread concern, and these issues underpin the expansion of publicly provided health insurance and are at the heart of the controversy. But the rationale for it is often not sufficiently contextualized with robust philosophical debate.

The contemporary American philosopher John Rawls asserted that social justice occurs when a distribution of wealth is allocated behind a veil of ignorance. He asks us to imagine a world where one is placed in a forum along with everyone else and nobody knows what wealth or abilities they or anybody else possesses. How would they then allocate? Rawls argues that a minimal but adequate level of welfare would be provided to all and that this should then be the basis for economic justice. The unique abilities of some in society should not be thwarted but should rather be employed to the benefit of all. In practice, that may mean high incomes for some but high taxation too. Justice implies that inequalities are organized to be mutually advantageous and that the world presents equal opportunity. In health-care, it may mean sufficient entitlement but not necessarily an equal one. A related school of thought, communitarianism, prioritizes the group rather than the individual, say, a family, church, city, state, or nation of which one is a member; the well-being of the group is transferred downward to the welfare of the individual. Within the group, social relations are stressed including socialized forms of healthcare.

Another important ethical issue concerns allocative efficiency. The COVID epidemic underscored tradeoffs between protecting the public and saving lives on the one hand versus economic activity, livelihoods, and per-sonal freedom on the other. Public health and progressive interest groups lean toward the former, while business and conservative groups lean toward the latter. Self-interest explains much of the posturing but there are impor-tant philosophical differences here. Many in the health sciences community believe it is unethical to limit care because of cost, or at least they prefer a very high threshold for denial of care, and they favor institutions that mini-mize the issue of cost. In their view, health is seen as a fundamental right consistent with human dignity for all. More market-minded people, however, such as those in business and economics, tend to take a utilitarian perspec-tive. Utilitarianism, articulated by John Stuart Mill in the 19th century, but with roots in epicureanism of antiquity, posits that individuals should have freedom to pursue their own happiness and that the greatest good results from a society of utility-maximizing citizens. Mill hoped that increasing abundance associated with economic development would lead to less mate-rialism and instead to the pursuit of higher pleasures including the arts, ath-letics, and intellectual pastimes. The greatest good for the greatest number, however, does not necessarily mean destitution for the least fortunate. Mill believed that we naturally have compassion for all of our fellow citizens and because of it, philanthropy would thrive under the utilitarian model, accom-modating the least fortunate as a matter of self-interest.

But the greatest good for the greatest number can adversely impact some groups, so much so as to violate basic rights. Therefore, utilitarian-ism must play out in a world ordered by rights and responsibilities, and this was recognized by Mill. Other philosophers, such as Immanuel Kant, emphasized human rights, responsibilities, and free agency. Individuals should be free from encroachment and harm by others. In this light, what are the rights of individuals and society to protection from a pandemic or other threats to health versus the right of the majority to pursue their lives to the fullest? There is a tradeoff that can be measured in terms of cost per quality-adjusted life year. Using this tradeoff model, how much economic output should we sacrifice to avert loss of life from infectious disease? Arguably, it should be consistent with decisions about other health intervention costs and benefits. So, for example, COVID intervention cost per quality-adjusted life year should not exceed that for influenza, cancer, or stroke. Yet, few advocates on either side of the debate embrace this explicit utilitarian approach with clear human rights impact. A reluctance to put a price on life may be part of the explanation. Politicians, in particular, tend to dodge such questions. But obfuscation of the tradeoffs and ethical underpinnings of policy decisions does not serve the greater public interest. More transparent and explicit decision-making would likely lead to more efficient and possibly equitable outcomes, and therefore policy reform to advance this transparency for the health sector is needed. For example, the Food and Drug Administration (FDA) could be given explicit responsibility for determining cost-effectiveness in addition to the safety and efficacy of new products. This would help public and private insurers improve allocative efficiency in coverage decisions. The FDA has thus far resisted stepping into this role.

The Challenges: Efficiency and Equity

The title of this book emphasizes the cost of healthcare in America, which is our biggest challenge going forward. To be sure, efficiency is not always about reducing costs; some costs, even high ones are worth it. But we should strive to produce health services at a minimum cost for a given level of quantity and quality. We should also be efficient in identifying what is not worth the cost. These two realms of productive and allocative efficiency constitute our primary challenge. Surveys show that Americans are well aware of the cost problem in healthcare and rank it among the most serious and important we face. Those working in the health sector tend to put less emphasis on the cost issue; after all, healthcare costs drive their incomes. Instead, they emphasize quality. Higher levels of quality, they argue, improve social well-being. It also tends to bolster their incomes when associated with higher costs. The status quo suits them and their rationale for staying the course is why external disruption, market-based or otherwise, is so important and necessary to meet the challenge of improving cost structure and rendering healthcare more efficient.

Equity is also important. It is a different kind of challenge, less technical and economic and more philosophical and social. It requires an awareness of economic justice, where a grounding in ethics and philosophy is helpful. One wonders if our increasingly vocationally oriented institutions of higher education are preparing the citizenry to reach well-informed decisions about such issues. Are Americans entitled to healthcare and if so, how much? Is it acceptable to have two or more tiers of health insurance? And then there are equity issues concerning finance; they include whether to continue to rely on employment-based financial contributions. This impacts labor markets and undermines efficiency as labor mobility is constrained by health insurance considerations. It also tends to be regressive since health insurance is a larger portion of the total earnings of lower-income households. And if health finance is tax-based, should it be derived from social security taxes (which are also regressive) or more general and commonly progressive taxation such as income taxes?

The United States has made great strides in expanding insurance coverage so that most of the population is insured. There are, however, about 10% of Americans who are not covered, as well as disparities in coverage and access. Progressive elements of society believe that having 90% of Americans insured is insufficient whatever the reason and they continue to call for universal coverage. But there is less consensus among them about how to get there. Not all who want universal coverage support single-payer healthcare because it would confer greater levels of government control and would bestow more market power to contain spending. Conservatives generally agree on some level of social assistance to provide a basic level of care to the deserving elements of society. But they differ on what a basic level of care entails and who are the deserving constituents targeted for help. There is no constitutional right to healthcare and there is discomfort among conservatives with large-scale entitlements, as they view them as weakening incentives to work and undermining individual character. Equity does not necessarily mean equal in their view, and they differ from progressives on what an equitable entitlement is. The resolution of these issues is primarily a political issue, not an economic one, and typically our political and judicial processes drive outcomes.

Beyond these conceptual and philosophical issues, we have more tangible challenges at hand. Our society is aging and our long-term care institutions are not always up to the task. Those with few assets in retirement may qualify for Medicaid, where reimbursement levels are low and, as a result, quality care is a challenge. The COVID pandemic exposed substandard nursing home care with high mortality rates. In addition, dementia in the US population is on the rise and long-term care for such patients is particularly problematic. Older persons with high net worth can afford to pay for what they need, but there is a segment in the middle class without the means to adequately cover long-term care expenses but with too much wealth to qualify for Medicaid. And then there is Medicare, where the Part A trust fund will be exhausted in just a few years. Yet, with ever more retirees relative to the working-age population, few in Washington are promoting a plan to address this issue. Will it be higher taxes, more constrained reimbursements, or reduced benefits? Alternatively, perhaps all Medicare financing will be shifted to general revenues, which would have serious implications for deficits and debt. This is a problem that must be addressed in the coming years.

We have seen that market power and monopolistic competition are widespread in the health sector. Much of this state of affairs is owing to an asymmetry of information. Although a more educated and informed consumer base incentivized by high deductible plans helps discipline the market and renders it more efficient, this can go only so far. For one thing, much healthcare occurs after deductibles are met, where consumers have little incentive to economize. For another, consumer-driven healthcare has had only mixed success amid poor price transparency thus far, and there is resistance to high deductible and tax-advantaged saving plans that are regressive. A lack of adequate cost accounting systems is an important part of the problem; providers do not even know what their costs are at the level of consumer pricing because their accounting systems do not provide this information. A better policy could direct healthcare providers, especially large ones, to shift away from reimbursement-driven accounting to more sound managerial accounting systems to better manage costs. Instead, many in the health sector would like to reverse the trend and move away from consumer-driven healthcare, which would undermine competitive pressures and increase reliance on nonmarket forms of rationing. Reducing consumer incentives will place a greater burden on the insurance industry to shop for more economical care, assuming they are subject to competitive pressures by employers and insurance beneficiaries.

The occupational control of healthcare is a leading concern, as we have seen, but now there appears to be bipartisan support for a loosening of the traditional models of education, training, and certification. Still, occupational control largely rests in state capitals, where there is often less transparency and more naked interest group politics. This poses a challenge to federal initiatives for reform. Successful reform is more likely if local and state activism influences policy-makers and that will require giving the issue greater public visibility.

The alternative to a more competitive approach is a greater role for the public sector. The movement toward a single-payer system, all-payer system, or public option would concentrate purchasing power, which could constrain costs more successfully than a dysfunctional free market if it can avoid capture by the industry to sustain high prices. But capture, as often occurs in regulated markets, may be of less risk here as legislatures and administrators have a keen interest in cost control and must balance health and nonhealth expenditures. The healthcare sector is also likely to be closely watched by the public. We observe more constrained spending elsewhere in the world where health expenditures as a share of GDP are lower, even with near-universal access to health services. It may not be possible to provide a consistent universal benefit unless it is sufficiently basic to be affordable. This problem would be larger in the absence of meaningful cost sharing. The affluent will tend to top up with supplemental insurance, possibly provided by private markets, when benefits are perceived to be too meager. Again, this is something we observe in other countries.

Single-payer health insurance will lower administrative costs and can use market power to constrain spending, but it may struggle to maintain dynamism and responsiveness to consumer demand in an environment of rapid change. On the other hand, insurers in well-designed all-payer systems have more incentives to manage care and compete for beneficiaries. All-payer systems, such as those found in Europe, retain a pluralistic system of multiple payers under the control of a governing body. All-payer systems often develop and enforce uniform payment rates to providers.

The Promise and Opportunity of the Health Sector

We have seen that productivity gains drive long-run prosperity. And we have seen that the health sector has been a drag on productivity gains and will become more serious as it becomes a larger part of the economy. The view taken here is that this course can be altered by means of institutional change and new technology. Reform that encourages competitive conditions where possible and better public sector oversight where they are not possible will bring about improvement, especially in the long run. A healthcare environment that is receptive to disruption of the status quo will be able to make good use of a wide range of new technologies, and they, in turn, will sustain the growth of healthcare as a leading sector of the economy and help define the future.

Healthcare information technology paired with artificial intelligence offers great promise. Information technology was advanced by the Community Reinvestment Act and the ACA, leading to the pervasive use of electronic health records, e-scheduling, and e-prescribing. This has improved the quality and convenience of care. And there is much more to come. Electronic health records can be used to improve diagnostics and treatment, especially when employed by sophisticated artificial intelligence applications. Wearable devices and cell phone applications can be paired with a consumer's health system to provide real-time monitoring of physiology including heart, lung, and blood functions. Monitoring can go beyond cell phone applications. Toilets can be equipped with sensors to monitor waste; and they can be linked to health system information technology to better identify cancer, renal activity, and other important functions. Artificial intelligence will soon aid radiologists and pathologists with their diagnostic interpretations. And at least some such advancement may become largely automated, substituting for expensive specialist physicians and other medical experts.

Effective healthcare technology does benefit from scale and scope, and this is problematic for competition. It drives the market toward greater levels of concentration as smaller organizations consolidate to better participate in new technology; it is a problem sure to be a concern of future antitrust policy work. Other problems of information technology implementation concern culture. Many providers, especially older ones, have been uncomfortable with major systemic changes and have been slow to adapt to them. User interface with IT is not always easy for providers or patients, and consequently continuous refinement is expected, particularly to empower consumers to better manage their own health. Data ownership is a problem too; as noted, healthcare organizations possess their patient data and are reluctant to share it. Data provides market power when less than fully fungible, and many healthcare systems have resisted joining health information exchanges to promote the easy transfer of data between separate organizations and healthcare systems. They do not want to encourage patients to switch providers. One important institutional change is the reform of data ownership to better empower consumers to easily move from one provider to another.

Other exciting technologies are just beginning to come to fruition. Three-dimensional printing provides better and faster medical and dental prosthetics. CRISPR, a gene editing technology, promises a wide range of better treatments. It has already led to advances in care for sickle cell anemia. New approaches to vaccine discovery, such as RNA messenger approaches that enabled the quick development of COVID vaccines, are a welcome development as are the innovations that led to effective vaccines for Ebola. A much better understanding of the ecology of the human digestive tract can be expected to emerge; it is another frontier of medicine and may yield important therapeutic results. And there is nanomedicine, focusing on the use of tiny sensors, instruments, and other devices to better understand and treat health conditions. It too is full of promise.

These and other technologies combined with the reform of occupational control, greater levels of competition in healthcare and better public oversight could herald a watershed change from stasis to a threshold of productivity gains, and at least in many cases, lower costs. It is probably too much to expect productivity gains of the magnitude seen in computers and electronic equipment where there was a five-fold gain from 1993 to 2007. But more modest achievement would still be of great importance both in the health sector and the wider economy.

Today, there are thousands of proprietary new medical products in development, and leading the pack are potential treatments for cancer, neurological disorders, infectious diseases, and immunological conditions. To be sure, successful products will be patent protected, conferring monopoly power, and they will be very expensive. Financial incentives for the development of new technology are important, of course, but economists have questioned the efficiency of our current patent regime. It is suboptimal and over-incentivizes. Levels of innovation could be largely sustained with alternative forms of incentivization such as prizes or grants that would economize on funds allocated. Better targeting of funds for innovation could employ greater numbers of researchers at the same cost and potentially generate greater output.

Patent reform to better optimize discovery and innovation with affordability is another issue ripe for institutional reform. There appears to be bipartisan support for some of this. We of course do not want to throw the baby out with the bathwater, and so such reform must be carefully crafted. For example, Figure 10.2 shows the progress made in treating a range of common forms of cancer. Five-year survival rates have improved markedly for most forms of cancer from the 1970s to the period of 2007–2013. We want this headway to continue. There is also the related problem of publicly funded research at universities and elsewhere fueling the development of private drugs and related products. Many critics see this as blatant private appropriation at public expense.

Five-year cancer survival rates in the USA

Average five-year survival rates from common cancer types in the United States,
shown as the rate over the period 1970-77 [●] and over the period 2007-2013 [●]: 1970-77 ●————►● 2007-2013
This five-year interval indicates the percentage of people who live longer than five years following diagnosis.

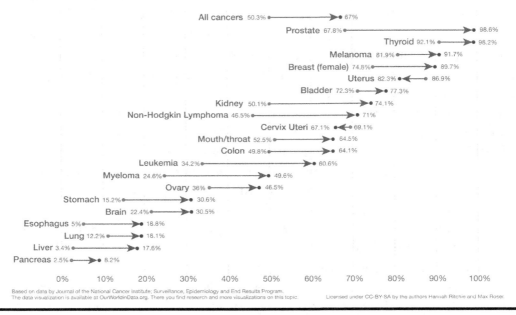

Figure 10.2   Improvement in Cancer Care

Source: https://ourworldindata.org/cancer-death-rates-are-falling-five-year-survival-rates-are-rising

Our World in Data

Cancer death rates are falling; five-year survival rates are rising

By Hannah Ritchie.

Reprinted with permission of Our World in Data.

Concluding Comments

Looking ahead into the immediate future, healthcare managers see much greater use of information technology paired with remote applications including wearable devices. Telemedicine is another major player, having broken out in a big way during the COVID epidemic. Greater use of such technology will be associated with more consolidation and the need for greater antitrust vigilance. More consumer participation with or without high deductibles is also a matter of considerable consensus among healthcare managers when they anticipate the broad changes that lie ahead. We may well witness a disruption of the prevailing models toward patients and away from providers, one that is expected to improve consumer and patient welfare. Problems will be seen as these changes occur: Cybersecurity has been highlighted along with the cost and scarcity of human resources needed to meet the demands of this rapidly evolving sector.

In my teaching, I have told students that the world they retire into will be very different from the one they experience today. Life expectancy will be much higher. People may routinely live beyond 100 years and demands on the health sector, accordingly, will be transformed. Better control of cardiovascular conditions, cancer, and dementia seems likely and other health conditions may evolve as important causes of morbidity and mortality. Technology and our institutions will evolve too with different roles for consumers, providers, and the state. I think how far healthcare has come since today's baby boomers were young. Telemedicine was in the realm of science fiction then as were many of today's noninvasive diagnostics and microtechnologies. The future is bound to be every bit as exciting and transformational.

Index

Note: Page numbers in italics indicate a figure on the corresponding page.

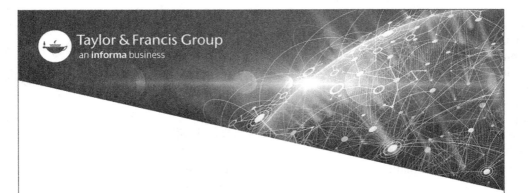

Taylor & Francis Group
an **informa** business

Taylor & Francis eBooks

www.taylorfrancis.com

A single destination for eBooks from Taylor & Francis
with increased functionality and an improved user
experience to meet the needs of our customers.

90,000+ eBooks of award-winning academic content in
Humanities, Social Science, Science, Technology, Engineering,
and Medical written by a global network of editors and authors.

TAYLOR & FRANCIS EBOOKS OFFERS:

A streamlined
experience for
our library
customers

A single point
of discovery
for all of our
eBook content

Improved
search and
discovery of
content at both
book and
chapter level

REQUEST A FREE TRIAL
support@taylorfrancis.com

Routledge
Taylor & Francis Group

CRC Press
Taylor & Francis Group